CHAPTER SIXTY+

FELICIA ZEVEN

CHAPTER SIXTY+

Heal, Transform, and Thrive After Your Sixties

---⊙⊙⊙---

A Therapeutic Toolkit for Emotional Healing
and Purposeful Living in your decades ahead

Self-published, 2025

Copyright © 2025 by Felicia Zeven

All rights reserved. No part of this publication may be reproduced, distributed, or transmitted in any form or by any means, including photocopying, recording, or other electronic or mechanical methods, without the prior written permission of the publisher.

First edition, 2025

Book cover design by Nika Eterovič

Published September 2025

ISBN paperback: 978-9090408958
ISBN e-book: 978-9090408972

Felicia Zeven
The Netherlands

www.chapter60.online (you can also find the worksheets here)

To all the clients I've had the privilege of meeting along the way:
Thank you for your trust, your courage,
and for sharing your stories with such honesty.
Your willingness to be vulnerable has been a constant
reminder of the strength that lives in the human spirit.

And to my family and my partner:
Thank you for cheering me on through every chapter,
both on the page and in life.

This isn't just a psychology book. It's a conversation. A journey. A therapeutic toolkit disguised as a warm, honest guide; written especially for those in their sixties, seventies, and beyond who are brave enough to ask:
what now?

TABLE OF CONTENTS

INTRODUCTION 11

PART ONE: Finding Your Way Back to Yourself 17

   CHAPTER 1: Why You Are Who You Are 19

   CHAPTER 2: The Here and Now 35

   CHAPTER 3: What's Holding You Back? 43

   CHAPTER 4: The Art of Making Peace 51

   CHAPTER 5: Rewriting Identity 65

   CHAPTER 6: The Courage to Change 77

PART TWO: The Realities of Later Life 85

   CHAPTER 7: Loss and Grief—Living with What Can't Be Fixed 89

   CHAPTER 8: Retirement—When the Alarm Clock Stops 95

   CHAPTER 9: Loneliness—And Why It Hurts So Much 101

   CHAPTER 10: This Body, Now—When Physical Changes Shake the Ground Beneath You 107

   CHAPTER 11: Bridging the Generational Gap 115

   CHAPTER 12: The Meaning of Life—A Conversation Worth Having 121

STORIES FROM THE THERAPY ROOM 129

AFTERWORD 147

INTRODUCTION

From me (a young psychologist) to you (someone brave enough to change at 60+).

So, you've bought this self-help book. First of all, thank you. Second of all, I can imagine what might've gone through your head when you did.

Is this really going to help me?
Am I falling for some clever marketing gimmick?
*And who is this woman, born in 1990 (go ahead, do the math), telling me **now** is the time to change my life?*

Let me introduce myself before we dive in. I'm a Dutch psychologist, and for many years, I worked with (mostly young) adults. People trying to figure out how to start their lives, including finding jobs, relationships, direction, and purpose. There is a lot of confusion, pressure, and inner drama. However, my career then took a different course. During an additional two-year training to become a licensed healthcare psychologist, I was asked to work with an entirely different group: older adults.

In the Netherlands, "older adults" refers to anyone over sixty-five. Suddenly, I wasn't talking to people preparing for their future, but rather to those looking back at their past. Instead of first steps, we were talking about "final chapters." And in those conversations, something stirred within me—a deeper respect, curiosity, and sense of purpose.

What I saw—and you might recognise this—was a generation raised with strength and silence. You weren't taught to talk about your feelings. You didn't grow up analysing your upbringing or reflecting on patterns. You worked hard, followed the rules, and built a life. For many of you, that life was okay, perhaps even good . . . but maybe not *completely* yours.

You might find yourself now with a bit more time, fewer responsibilities, and a quieter house—but also with a body that's not as energetic, a mind that sometimes races, and memories that stir up emotions you didn't expect to be still carrying. Regrets, old conflicts, unresolved dreams, and grief. Patterns that feel too ingrained to change. But here's the truth: **it's never too late**.

I've helped clients in their sixties, seventies, and even eighties make incredible shifts—not by reinventing their entire lives, but by gently *untangling* the threads that no longer serve them. We explored why they became the way they are, how they formed certain beliefs and habits, and what they could still do to change, live with more peace, more freedom, and, yes, even more joy.

This book is a carefully crafted guide built on ten years of clinical experience, countless training hours, and hundreds of honest, raw, and powerful conversations with clients. It contains bite-sized lessons in psychology, practical exercises, and thought-provoking reflections. Many of the exercises have their origin in evidence-based approaches, such as cognitive behavioural therapy (CBT), acceptance and commitment therapy (ACT), narrative therapy, and positive psychology. You can work through it alone or with someone you trust. You can go fast or slow. But whatever pace you take, *you'll be taking steps forward.*

The way I speak to you here is exactly how I speak in the therapy room: clear, curious, a bit playful when it fits, but always deeply respectful of your story. I love explaining *why* we do specific exercises or look at certain patterns—because I don't just want you to follow along. I want you to *understand*. To connect the dots. To feel ownership of your own process.

Part one of the book is structured in the same way I'd structure a series of ten to twenty therapy sessions, if we were sitting across from each other every week. That means it starts with **building the foundation**: *Who are you? Why do you think, feel, and act the way you do? What has shaped you—your history, your character, your experiences?* Once that groundwork is laid, we move into **what might be holding you back**. The hidden beliefs, the patterns, the inner voice that whispers just loud enough to keep you stuck. I'll guide you through understanding them— not with judgement, but with clarity and compassion.

From there, we shift toward **strengthening your identity**. We'll explore who you are *now*, what you still value, and how you want to show up. Especially later in life, identity can begin to blur. Things change. Roles fall away. But that doesn't mean you're done growing. Reconnecting with your sense of self is not just empowering—it's necessary. And finally, we move into **action**. Tools. Practices. Realistic ways to shift your mindset, your energy, your days.

Part two of this guide explores some of the most common themes I encounter in therapy with individuals at this stage of life, including retirement, grief, and loneliness. I've included these chapters to help you recognise that you're not alone in facing these challenges. I hope that by reading them, you'll feel seen, understood, and gently reminded that many others quietly wrestle with the same questions and emotions.

That said, I'm a very hands-on psychologist. I believe insight is power, but transformation comes from action. This isn't a guide to read and nod along with while sipping your morning coffee (though, let's be honest, that's not a bad way to begin). But real, lasting change? That takes more than just understanding. Let each chapter sink in. Sit with the questions, even the *uncomfortable* ones. I would recommend that you get a notebook and write things down—thoughts, memories, answers to the exercises, feelings you didn't expect to have. Writing things down doesn't just help you remember—it enables you to make sense. It unscrambles what's in your head, and once something has words, it becomes something you can work with. Reflect, write, re-read. Don't rush it. Be honest with yourself. Because this isn't just about fixing problems—it's about giving yourself the gift of a more peaceful, more intentional, more *you* version of your life.

INTRODUCTION

Why did I create this? Because therapy is not always accessible, waiting lists are long, and sessions can be expensive. This is my way of giving you the tools I wish more people had access to. Also, because I know that growth belongs not only to the young; it belongs to the willing. If this guide can help just one person feel more alive, more peaceful, more themselves, it will have been worth every minute of writing.

And just so you know, your purchase is part of something bigger than this book. It helps me continue creating work that uplifts, encourages, and inspires others to chase their dreams and believe in themselves. From my heart to yours, thank you for being part of this journey.

Now, let's get started.

This might not be the beginning of your life, but it can absolutely be the beginning of a new chapter.

And I promise . . . it's going to be a good one.

Warmly,
Your (slightly younger) psychologist

PART ONE:
Finding Your Way Back to Yourself

FELICIA ZEVEN

CHAPTER SIXTY+

CHAPTER 1:
Why You Are Who You Are

Or: How Your Brain Became the Filter You Didn't Know You Were Wearing

Let's take a moment to get personal. Not just about you, but about *how all of us*—yes, even your seemingly put-together neighbour with the shiny hedges and her daily Nordic walk—came to be the way we are.

As a psychologist, I can tell you this: you didn't just magically become *you*. You were shaped, formed, influenced, bumped, bruised, loved, hurt, praised, ignored, hugged, judged, and taught—from the day you were born until . . . well, last week probably. And if you've ever wondered, *Why do I keep reacting this way?* or *Why does life feel so heavy sometimes?* this chapter is for you.

Let me break it down for you. Psychologically speaking, there are **three major forces** that shape how you see the world and yourself. Think of them as three giant **input streams** feeding into your inner system: your *upbringing*, your (personal) *experiences*, and your *character*.

1. Your Upbringing: The First Lenses You Ever Wore (And Probably Still Are)

Imagine your mind as a pair of lenses. The very first pair you were ever handed came from your upbringing—your parents, caregivers, teachers, the adults around you. These people passed down **values, beliefs, and unwritten rules**—sometimes with love, sometimes with stress, and sometimes while just trying to survive their own lives.

If your parents valued independence, you may have learned: *Don't be a burden.*

If they avoided emotions, you may have picked up: *Keep your feelings to yourself.*

If they were very controlling, perhaps you learned: *If I want to feel safe, I need to be in control.*

And if they were loving but inconsistent, you may have felt: *I need to earn love by being perfect.*

This marks the beginning of what psychologists refer to as **core beliefs**: deep, often unconscious rules and assumptions about life. And those become the lenses you wear. You don't *see* the lenses; you see *through* them. And unless you stop and clean them off (or maybe even change prescriptions), they'll quietly guide your life for decades.

What's interesting is that as we grow up, we usually go one of two ways:

1. **We copy parts of our parents or caregivers** ("Wow, I *am* turning into my mother"), or

2. **We do the complete opposite out of rebellion or survival.**

But in both cases, we're still responding to the same original script. It's just a remix.

2. Your Life Experiences:
The Stories You Never Chose, But Carry Anyway

Now let's add another layer: **your life experiences**. Childhood bullying, early heartbreak, grief, family conflict, betrayal, abuse, illness, world events, economic hardship—the big and the small all leave fingerprints on your nervous system and mind.

Some of these moments you remember clearly. Others are more vague, but still live inside you. And they teach you things. Not always the right things, but powerful things about yourself and others:

- *People leave.*
- *I'm not good enough.*
- *The world isn't safe.*
- *If I don't do everything perfectly, something bad will happen.*

Even global events like the COVID-19 pandemic, wars, and economic instability can profoundly shape how safe you feel in the world, and whether the future feels open or terrifying. When you've lived long enough, these experiences start to pile up. You may not talk about them often, but they sit there quietly, influencing how much joy or fear you allow yourself to feel.

3. Your Own Nature: DNA, Temperament, and the Beautiful You

Let's not forget that you entered this world with your unique characteristics. Some of us are born with a more sensitive nervous system, while others are born with more fire or boldness. Some people are naturally cautious; others are adventurous. And this temperament interacts with your environment from the very beginning.

It's not just *what* happened to you . . . it's also *how you experienced it*.

A naturally anxious child in a chaotic home might become hypervigilant and emotionally withdrawn. A bold child in a strict household might become rebellious or overly self-critical.

So:

- Your **upbringing** laid the foundation.
- Your **life experiences** added texture (and probably a few scars).

- And your **personality** filtered and reacted to all of it in a way only *you* could.

That's your **input**.

The Output: How All That Input Shapes You Today

Now that we've explored the *input*—your upbringing, life experiences, and personality—it's time to look at what that input creates: **your output**.

In other words, *how you think, feel, and behave today.*

Think of yourself as a beautiful, complicated machine. What goes in (experiences, messages, habits, stress, love, trauma) affects what comes out (thoughts, reactions, expectations, emotions). Most of it happens quietly, behind the scenes, without you even noticing it.

Let's break the output into three essential areas of your life:

1. How You See Yourself

Who am I, really?

This is where it all gets personal. How you see yourself—your identity, self-worth, personality, preferences—is *profoundly shaped* by everything you've taken in over the years.

Your upbringing may have taught you what was "good" or "bad" about being *you*. Maybe you were told you were too sensitive. Or not smart enough. Or always needed to be the strong one. Over time, these ideas became internalised. Not just *what happened to you*, but what you *took from it.*

Ask yourself honestly:

- *Who am I?*
- *What do I like? What do I avoid?*
- *Why do I keep doubting myself even when I've achieved so much?*
- *Why do I feel guilty when I rest?*

The answers are rarely just personality traits. If you struggle with low self-esteem, indecisiveness, or feeling *not enough*, know this: they're shaped by decades of messages you've received directly or indirectly—whether through praise, criticism, neglect, comparison, or even silence. Some of these messages are outdated. Some are lies you believed to protect yourself. And some are life rules you formed in silence.

2. How You See the Future

Is there anything left for me?

This one can feel especially heavy as we age. For some, the future feels like a blank page—open and freeing. But for many, it starts to feel like a closed book, or worse, a ticking clock.

You might find yourself thinking:

- *What's the point of starting something new now?*

- *It's too late for significant changes.*
- *I've already missed my chance.*

However, these beliefs don't stem from truth—they stem from experience. If your past was marked by loss, disappointment, or unmet needs, your brain may attempt to protect you by lowering your expectations. It whispers: *Don't get your hopes up. Just accept how things are.*

Add to that the real-life challenges of ageing, including declining health, grief, loneliness, retirement, and changing roles. It's understandable that the future feels uncertain. But here's the truth: **even if life looks different now, it's not over.**

You still have time to:

- Change an inner belief that's been holding you back
- Create meaningful moments
- Heal something old
- Discover what peace and joy mean *to you*

The future isn't just about "what's left to do," but about *how you want to feel*. And you *can* feel something new, even now.

3. How You See the World (And the People in It)

Here's where your assumptions about others, society, and human nature start to show. Often, they form from years of accumulated experiences—and they shape how much connection or isolation you feel in your daily life.

Do any of these sound familiar?

- *People don't really care.*
- *If I show my true self, they'll judge me.*
- *Everyone else has it more together than I do.*
- *The world is going downhill.*

It's easy to start filtering everything through fear, shame, comparison, guilt, resentment, or cynicism—especially if you've been hurt or disappointed many times. And let's be honest, the world *has* shown some frightening sides: pandemics, war, polarisation, and economic instability.

But it's important to remember that these lenses, too, were shaped. You didn't choose to become mistrustful or guarded. These were protective strategies—learned over time.

Here's the problem: when you see the world as cold or dangerous, it can push you into **emotional isolation** . . . and loneliness only deepens the beliefs you started with.

It All Adds Up: Why This Matters

So let's zoom out for a second.

- **Upbringing**, **experiences**, and **temperament** shape what you believe.

- These beliefs influence how you **see yourself**, your **future**, and the **world**.

- And from there, you make choices—about what's possible, what you deserve, and what you avoid.

And this happens for decades, mostly on *autopilot*.

But you're not stuck. Because once you start to understand your internal *system*, you can begin to change it.

The Life Rules Built to Protect You—Now Blocking You

By now, you've probably started to see that your thoughts and behaviours didn't come from nowhere. They were shaped by **what life gave you and what it didn't**. Over time, your brain did something incredibly clever: it created **rules**.

Not written-down rules. Not even the rules you consciously remember agreeing to. But psychological survival rules. Quiet, powerful, and often invisible.

We call these **life rules**. And they tend to sound like this:

- *I must always stay in control.*

- *I shouldn't need help.*

- *I can't show weakness.*

- *If I make a mistake, I'll be judged.*

- *If I'm not useful, I'm not lovable.*

- *Good things don't last, so don't get too comfortable.*

You didn't invent these rules because you're dramatic. You invented them because you were *human* and probably trying to protect yourself from something painful. That's what these rules do: they offer safety, structure, predictability.

Let me give you a few real-life examples:

- If you cried as a child and no one came to comfort you, your brain might have built the rule:

"I have to deal with things on my own."

- If you only got praise when you performed well, you might now carry:

"I must always strive to be worthy."

- If someone close to you abandoned you, physically or emotionally, you might live by:

"Don't get too close to anyone—people leave."

These rules *worked*. They helped you navigate school, work, marriage, parenting, and life. They gave you a way to feel competent, safe, and even strong. That's why, for a long time, they didn't feel like *problems*. They felt like the *only way to be*.

But here's the twist:

What once helped you **survive** might now be stopping you from truly **living**.

The trouble begins when different life rules start contradicting each other or when they no longer fit the reality you're living in.

Let's say:

- You have a rule that says, *I must always be strong.*
- But you also sincerely want more emotional connection with your loved ones.

Or:

- You live by the principle that says, *I must always be productive to have value.*
- But your body is ageing, your energy isn't what it used to be, and rest feels necessary, yet you feel guilty.

Or:

- You've lived with *I can't depend on anyone.*
- But now you actually *need* support due to illness or grief, and you find it unbearably difficult to ask for it.

This is what psychologists call **internal conflict**: when two important values or beliefs pull you in opposite directions. The result? Exhaustion. Self-doubt. Shame. Feeling stuck. Or like something is *off*, but you can't quite name it.

It's Not About Blame. It's About Understanding.

Now, before your inner critic kicks in—*I should've figured this out by now!*—take a breath. This isn't about blaming yourself, your parents, or your past.

It's about **bringing things into awareness**. You can't change what you can't see. Seeing these life rules clearly and naming them is the first step toward loosening their grip.

Because while those rules once protected your most vulnerable parts, they're no longer the only option. You can create new ways of being. Gentler ways. More honest ways. And that's precisely what this process is for.

Exercise 1.1 | Your life, Laid Out

Before we proceed, we need to pause and take a look back. Not just quickly, not just in your head, but *on paper*.

This might be the most emotionally demanding part of the entire guide. But it's also one of the most powerful. To understand why you are who you are today, we need to take a compassionate and honest look at where you've been.

You have **two options. Choose** whichever suits you best:

Option 1: Write Your Life Story

Grab a notebook or open a blank document. Start writing about your life, from your earliest memories until now. Don't worry about grammar, perfection, or style. This isn't a novel—it's a self-exploration.

Include:

- Key memories
- Turning points
- Challenges, losses, heartbreaks
- Moments of joy, pride, or unexpected strength
- People who shaped you—for better or worse

Let the words flow. You can write it all in one go or do it in pieces.

Option 2: Draw a Life Timeline

If writing freely feels overwhelming, make a **timeline of your life**. Start from birth on the left and move to the present on the right. Mark:

- Major events (positive and negative)
- High points (achievements, moments of love, milestones)
- Low points (loss, trauma, illness, hardship)
- Transitions (new jobs, relationships, children, retirement, etc.)

You can keep it simple or add notes to each moment.

Why Include the Highs?

It's easy to focus only on what went wrong. But **your highs matter just as much**.

They show your **strength**, your **resilience**, your **capacity for joy**. They remind you that pain isn't the only thing that shaped you—**hope, love, and success did, too.**

Exercise 1.2 | Reflection:
Ask yourself these questions

After writing your story or drawing your timeline, sit with these questions. Answer the ones that resonate. Skip and return as needed. This is *your* process.

1. What life events shaped me into who I am today?
2. What did I learn from those events—about myself, about others, or about how life works?
3. Which of those lessons became life rules I still follow (consciously or not)?
4. What pain am I still carrying with me today?
5. Have I ever felt like I had to be someone I wasn't in order to survive or be accepted?
6. What patterns do I keep repeating in relationships, habits, or self-talk?
7. What beliefs do I hold about myself that might no longer be true?
8. When in my life did I feel truly proud, powerful, or at peace?
9. Who or what have I not forgiven (including myself)?
10. What am I still curious about, still longing for, or still wanting to change—even now?

Purpose of this groundwork:

This exercise is not about digging up pain just for the sake of it, but about **gaining insight** into what shaped your identity—and beginning to challenge what no longer serves you gently. Psychologists often refer to this as your **"narrative identity,"** a kind of internal story you've written about yourself over the years. This story shapes your choices, emotions, self-talk, and beliefs about what is or isn't possible. And it quietly influences your day-to-day life, often without you even being aware of it.

When you see your life laid out, you'll start to recognise:

- The **themes** that keep coming back
- The **beliefs** you've internalised
- The **strengths** you've built through survival
- The **unfinished stories** you're still carrying

This reflection isn't just powerful—**it's foundational**.

Everything that follows in this guide will build on what you uncover here. So take your time. Be honest. Be kind. And remember, this is just the *beginning*.

CHAPTER 2:
The Here and Now

In the previous chapter, we explored how your early environment, your life experiences, and your unique personality have all contributed to the person you've become. We examined the concept of input—everything that shaped you—and output, how those influences manifest in your behaviour, beliefs, and emotional responses today.

You've taken a trip through your past. Perhaps you wrote your life story, or maybe you stared at a timeline full of memories—the beautiful, the painful, the ones that still sting, and the ones that warm your heart. If you actually did the work, well done. Truly.

Now, we land in the present.

Because everything you explored—the values passed down by your parents, your early emotional experiences, the expectations you absorbed from school, culture, or religion, the things life threw your way (both your fault and not)—*all of it* shaped how you've ended up living today.

You might be starting to realise just how much of your life has been running on autopilot—unspoken expectations, silent rules, and learned habits. Maybe some of them served you well. Maybe others kept you stuck. Either way, they brought you **here**, to this very moment.

Why the Present Moment Matters

In therapy, we often describe the present as your *launchpad*.

Not because it's where your story began, or where it will end, but because it's the only place where **you can actually do something**.

You are living with the consequences of your past choices, your environment, your coping mechanisms, your relationships, and sometimes, of things you never chose at all. But the beauty of the present is this: it gives you the chance to ask, *Do I still want to carry this with me?*

Here's the thing: many people avoid examining their current life closely. Because the moment you look, you might have to feel. Then soon after, you might have to confront grief, regret, boredom, resentment, loneliness, or maybe just the quiet sadness that things didn't turn out quite how you imagined. Getting older brings a whole new wave of identity questions. Retirement shifts your sense of purpose. Losses challenge your emotional balance. Your changing body affects your independence. And a lifetime of habits suddenly gets put under the microscope.

It's easy to start believing that you're "done," that your identity is fixed, your patterns are permanent, and that change is for the young. But as a professional who has walked this path with many others, let me reassure you: **it's never too late to come home to yourself.** I'll guide you through a few simple but powerful exercises to help you make sense of where you are right now. This is the beginning of building clarity, intention, and direction for what comes next.

Exercise 2.1 | The mirror Check-in

This one is simple, but powerful. Each morning (or evening, if you prefer), stand in front of a mirror and take a moment to truly see yourself. Not just your face, but the energy, the expression, the years behind your eyes. Then answer these three questions in your head:

How am I feeling today—emotionally and physically?
What do I need right now that I've been ignoring?
What is one small act of care or intention I can offer myself today?

You can do this daily or just a few times a week. The purpose is to create a regular moment of self-contact. To remember that your inner world matters, even on the quiet or busy days. In fact, it's one of my *favourite* exercises to give to clients because it creates a small but powerful moment of mindful self-connection. It's short, practical, and has the potential to shift your entire day into a more thoughtful and intentional direction. It helps you reconnect with yourself, even if just for sixty seconds.

Exercise 2.2 | The Three mirrors of the present moment

To truly meet yourself in the present, you need to look into three "mirrors":

1. The Mirror of Self

- How do I see myself at this moment?

- Do I like who I've become, or do I feel like I've lost touch with myself?

- What parts of me are still active, still vibrant, still curious?

- How do I talk to myself when I make mistakes?

- How do I treat myself on hard days?

This encompasses your self-image, self-esteem, and your relationship with your own needs and emotions.

2. The Mirror of the Future

- When I think about what's ahead, do I feel hopeful? Or uncertain—or maybe even fearful?

- Do I believe there's *still time* for me to change, grow, enjoy, heal?

- Do I secretly feel like "it's too late," or that certain dreams no longer belong to me?

Therapy teaches us that our view of the future reflects how much we still believe in ourselves and our capacity to make choices. This is especially important as we age—because while some chapters may close, others may still be waiting to open.

3. The Mirror of the World

- How do I relate to others these days?

- Do I assume people won't understand me—or do I still feel seen and heard?

- Do I compare myself to others and feel less than?

- Do I carry guilt, shame, or unresolved conflict in my relationships?

Your **worldview** shapes your sense of belonging, connection, and trust. And as we get older, relationships shift: kids grow up, partners may pass away, and friendships evolve. This mirror deserves attention, too.

Exercise 2.3 | Me then, me now

This exercise helps you reconnect with the dreams and ideas you once had about life—before life *got in the way*. It's not meant to make you feel regret. It's about understanding how your identity, desires, and expectations evolved, and what that means for the person you are today.

Step 1: Revisit Your Younger Self

Close your eyes and imagine yourself as a child—maybe seven, maybe ten. See their face, their clothes, their energy. Now answer these questions, writing them down in the voice or memory of your younger self:

- What did I want to be when I grew up?
- What did I love doing most?
- What kind of adult did I think I'd become?
- What did I believe about love, success, or happiness?
- What made me feel special or hopeful?

Step 2: Reflect on Your Current Self

Now, from the "you" of today, reflect on these:

- What (career) path did I follow?
- Who am I now?

- What are my beliefs about myself?
- What do I value?
- What is my social world like—am I connected, alone, appreciated?

Step 3: Compare

Look at the gap between your child self and your present self.

- Is the gap large or small?
- Are there dreams you carried through?
- Which dreams faded—and why?
- How do you feel about where you ended up?

CHAPTER 3:
What's Holding You Back?

By now, you've started reflecting on your life, reconnecting the dots with the "now," and maybe seeing some things in a new light. This next chapter is about something a little more tender. A bit closer to the bone. Let's talk about what **gets in the way** of change.

Because even when we *want* to grow, even when we say, *Alright, I'm ready*, something inside us still pulls the handbrake. We retreat. We freeze. We stay small. And most of the time, we don't even realise we're doing it.

In therapy, we refer to these internal blockages as such. In everyday language? The voice in your head that whispers, *You can't*, *What's the point?* or *You've missed your chance*. Let's break this down.

Part 1: Your Inner Dialogue – How Thoughts Shape Your Day

There's a reason one small thought can make your stomach twist or your motivation disappear. That's because thoughts, especially automatic ones, are compelling. And most of the time, they don't even feel like thoughts. They feel like the **truth**.

Here's how it works: **something happens → your brain produces an automatic thought** (often shaped by past experiences) **→ that thought triggers a feeling → and that feeling pushes you toward a specific behaviour**. I will give you a simple example:

Let's say you've always felt like your opinion wasn't valued in your family. Now, even as an adult, when someone interrupts you, your brain quickly fires off the thought: *See? What I say doesn't matter.*

You might not even notice the thought consciously, but you'll **feel** it—maybe sadness, or frustration, or shame.

And then comes the behaviour: you go quiet, or withdraw, or over-explain.

And just like that, you're back in a **pattern** that keeps your world small.

This is why understanding your **inner self-talk** is so important. The words you use with yourself—harsh, dismissive, fear-based—can slowly chip away at your confidence. You might stop trying new things, avoid people, procrastinate on dreams, or distract yourself endlessly.

And after a while, it begins to *feel like this is just who you are.*

Part 2: The Patterns You've Been Repeating

Let's go a layer deeper.

Sometimes, it's not just a single thought that holds us back; it's a whole pattern—a default setting. In psychology, we refer to them as **schemas**, but let's not get too clinical. Think of them as emotional "templates" that your brain created a long time ago—based on the people who raised you, the experiences you had, and what you needed (or didn't get).

They become the lens through which you interpret new experiences.

Here's the tricky part: these patterns are often *so familiar* that they feel safe, even if they're painful.

You may find yourself consistently taking on the caretaker role, prioritising others' needs and never fully expressing your own. Or maybe you isolate yourself because deep down you believe **you're a burden**. Or perhaps you chase **perfection and control**, terrified that if you let go, everything will fall apart.

These are not random behaviours. They're **survival strategies**. These patterns become **your default reactions**, especially in emotionally charged situations. They show up fast—faster than your thinking brain can catch them—and they often push you into one of two familiar *modes.*

And Then Come the Modes . . .

When one of these old emotional patterns (schemas) gets triggered—often without us even realising it—we automatically shift into what we call a **mode**.

Think of a mode as a **temporary emotional state** that takes over how you feel, think, and behave in that moment. It's like an old role you slip into without meaning to. You can think of it as a "you" from the past taking the wheel, while the present-day, grounded version of you gets pushed aside for a bit.

Modes are your brain's way of coping when an old wound feels touched. They're not random. They emerge from the deeper life patterns we've just discussed. So if you've carried a belief like *I'm not important*, your mode might be to withdraw, shut down, or go into people-pleasing. If your pattern is, *I must be in control to be safe*, your mode might be overly critical, rigid, or anxious.

There are many ways we can name and categorise modes in therapy, but to make things simple and practical, let's focus on two common ones:

a. The Inner Child Mode

This mode holds your unmet emotional needs: comfort, love, validation, and safety. When it gets activated, you might feel sad, helpless, rejected, anxious, or ashamed. You might avoid confrontation, isolate yourself, or feel overwhelmed by emotions that feel "too big" for the situation at hand.

b. The Inner Parent Mode

This is the voice of internalised criticism, high expectations, or even punishment. It can sound like: *You should know better by now.*

- *Don't be so weak.*
- *You're never going to get it right.*

Sometimes, this mode turns on others, and you become controlling, impatient, or even cold. But more often, it turns inward, causing shame, guilt, or pressure.

These modes aren't your enemies. They developed to get you through situations where you didn't have better tools available. But now that you do—or rather now that you're learning them—it's time to become aware of when they show up. Not to shut them down, but to gently say:

"Thank you for trying to protect me. But I've got this now."

The more you recognise these emotional shifts, the more space you create for your **Healthy Adult Mode**, the part of you that can respond with clarity, kindness, and wisdom.

You'll have the opportunity to explore this further in the upcoming exercises.

Exercise 3.1 | The thought tracker

This is one of the most powerful tools I give to clients. It might look simple, but don't underestimate it. You're about to become a private detective in your own mind. This exercise helps you catch the **automatic thoughts** you tell yourself and see how they shape your emotions and behaviour.

We often live on autopilot. We feel bad, irritated, low, or anxious . . . but we don't pause to ask: **"What did I just tell myself?"**

Start with this tracker. Print out the worksheet (www.chapter60.online) or write it in a notebook. Use it daily or whenever a strong emotion hits. Over time, patterns will start to emerge.

Situation (What happened?)	Automatic Thought (What did I say to myself?)	Emotion (What did I feel?)	Behaviour (What did I do next?)
Example: I forgot to call my daughter back.	"I always mess up. I'm a bad parent."	Guilt, shame, anxiety	Didn't call her back at all. Distracted myself with TV.

After a few days or a week of tracking, go back and reflect:

- Are there certain thoughts that repeat themselves?
- Do you notice that certain emotions come up more than others?
- Are your behaviours helping you or pulling you further away from what you want?

Exercise 3.2 | pattern spotting - Which mode am i in?

This exercise helps you uncover the deeper emotional patterns or "modes" you slip into—especially under stress, conflict, or when you feel overwhelmed.

Step 1: Think of a recent moment when you felt very emotionally reactive.

It could be anger, shame, withdrawal, people-pleasing—anything where you felt you weren't really choosing your behaviour but were just . . . reacting.

Write it down:

- What happened?
- How did you feel?
- What did you think?
- What did you do or say?

Step 2: Identify the Mode

Now, ask yourself: **Which mode was I in?**

- ◆ **Child Mode**

    - I felt small, rejected, helpless, or unworthy.
    - I just wanted someone to comfort me or "fix it."
    - I felt like giving up or pleasing others to keep the peace.

- **Parent Mode**
  - I was hard on myself or others.
  - I felt angry, controlling, critical, or frustrated.
  - I thought things like, "This is your fault" or "You need to be stronger."

- **Healthy Adult Mode** (less common in automatic reactions)
  - I was able to stay calm and reflective.
  - I could see both sides and respond with intention.
  - I showed compassion toward myself or someone else.

We often switch between modes in the same situation. That's okay—just notice what's dominant.

Step 3: Shift into Adult Mode (optional bonus)

Imagine you could go back to that situation. What would your **Healthy Adult self** say or do instead?

- What would they remind you?
- How would they respond to the inner child or quiet the inner critic?

Write a few sentences. Don't worry if it feels awkward at first—this is a skill you're building.

CHAPTER 4:
The Art of Making Peace

In this chapter, we will explore three themes that quietly shape the emotional landscape of later life: regret, acceptance versus change, and the concept of a **Circle of Influence**. Each one touches a different part of your inner world; from the weight of past choices, to the struggle of knowing when to act and when to let go, to understanding what's truly within your control. These are not easy topics, but they are essential if we want to live with more *peace*, *clarity*, and *intention* in the years ahead. Let's take them one by one.

Part 1: Regret—Learning to Live with the Unfinished

Let's be honest: regret is the heavy backpack many people carry around by the time they hit their sixties, seventies, or beyond. And it's not filled with random things either. It's usually packed with particular, sharp-edged memories:

I should have left earlier.

I wish I'd spoken up.
Why didn't I spend more time with them?
I wasted so much energy on things that didn't matter.

And here's the thing: *regret is completely human.* It means you've lived, made choices, loved, lost, missed chances, taken risks, or not taken them. It means you've accumulated a life full of moments that mattered to you.

But regret also has a sneaky side. Left unchecked, it becomes a kind of emotional quicksand. It can trap you in loops of *what if,* drain your energy, and distract you from the time and life that's still right in front of you. I see this in so many clients: the weight of old decisions, missed opportunities, or strained relationships holding them back like an invisible leash. And the worst part? Regret often comes with a second layer: *shame or guilt.* As if feeling bad about it once wasn't enough.

The Psychological Impact

From a psychological perspective, regret isn't just a passing feeling; it's an emotional experience that can profoundly affect how you think about yourself and your life. It fuels negative self-talk, reinforces unhelpful beliefs like *I always mess things up* or *I'm too late now.* It keeps your brain stuck in reverse gear while the rest of the world moves on.

And often, regret isn't just about a single event. It becomes part of a story you tell yourself about who you are: *I'm the one who failed, I missed my chance,* or *I hurt people and can't undo it*. These beliefs don't just hurt; they quietly **dictate your choices today**.

So, What Can You Do with It?

This may surprise you, but the goal isn't to erase regret. You can't. We don't have a rewind button (believe me, I would've pressed it by now, too). But what you *can* do is **shift your relationship with it**.

Here's how:

- **Look at it clearly.** What exactly are you regretting? Is it something you did or didn't do? What was in your control at the time, and what wasn't? Often, we judge our past selves with the wisdom we only gained *after* the fact.

- **Ask what it's teaching you.** Regret has a lesson in it. Maybe about your values. Your priorities. Your capacity to grow. What is the regret pointing you toward now?

It is not just about *thinking* differently; it's also about *doing* something that helps your mind, your body, and your heart loosen that grip. And that is why I would like to introduce a couple of powerful exercises:

Exercise 4.1 | Writing a letter

Healing regret often starts with something deceptively simple: putting words to what you've been carrying. That's what this exercise is all about. A letter. Not just any letter—but one with a purpose: to give voice to what was never said, never explained, or never forgiven. Depending on where your regret or guilt is focused, you can choose between two kinds of letters:

Option 1: A Letter to Your Former Self

We often hold ourselves hostage for choices we made when we knew less, had fewer tools, or were simply trying to survive. But here's the truth: the person you were back then wasn't the person you are now. They were doing their best with what they had. This letter is your chance to speak to that younger version of you. To offer understanding, kindness, and maybe even an apology.

How to Do It:

1. **Pick a "version" of yourself to write to:**

    Was it you at twenty? Thirty-five? Fifty? Choose the age or life phase where you feel a strong sense of regret or a significant moment that shaped you.

2. **Start your letter gently:**

    Use a tone you would use toward a friend or a loved one. You might begin with:

    "I've been thinking about you lately . . ." "I know you were trying your best . . ."

    "There's something I've never told you . . ."

3. **Include these elements:**

    o   What you remember about how you felt back then

    o   What you were going through or struggling with

    o   What you wish you could say now, with the wisdom and kindness you've gained

    o   Forgiveness or understanding, if you're ready

    By writing to your past self, you're not erasing what happened. You're acknowledging it, integrating it, and giving it a different ending, one that allows you to move forward with more softness and less shame.

Option 2: A Letter to Someone Else (Living or Gone)

Maybe your regret involves someone else. Something you said, or didn't say. A relationship that drifted, a wound that never closed, or a goodbye you never got to give. Whether that person is still in your life, long gone, or out of reach, writing a letter can bring surprising clarity and peace.

You don't have to send it. You don't even need them to read it. This is about *you* taking responsibility for your story. You might include:

- What you wish you'd said
- What you now realize about them or yourself
- Any apology, anger, or grief that still needs a voice
- What you would say now if you could

Yes, this might stir up emotions. That's okay. That's part of *grieving*. Let yourself feel what you feel. That's not a weakness. That's healing.

Option 3: What If You Want to Talk in Real Life?

Sometimes, writing it down is enough. But other times, you might feel a deeper pull — a sense that you want to actually *talk* to the person involved. Maybe to clear the air, to reconnect, or to finally say something that was never said. If that's where your heart is leaning, here's a little guidance from me — as a psychologist, and someone who's witnessed how powerful these conversations can be (and how scary they might feel too).

Tips for the Conversation Itself:

Keep it simple and honest. You don't need to deliver a speech. Try to speak from your own perspective. Say "I felt..." rather than "You made me...". That invites connection instead of defense. And above all, be okay with not knowing how it'll go. Sometimes the beauty of these moments isn't in what the other person says—it's in you showing up as the person you've become.

A Few Things to Consider Before You Reach Out:

- **What is your intention?**

    Ask yourself honestly: *Do I want to be heard? To apologize? To reconnect?* Being clear on what *you* hope for can help you enter the conversation grounded, not reactive.

> - **Are they open to talking?**
>
>   Some people need time. Some aren't ready. And some may not respond the way you hope. That doesn't mean your effort was wrong — it just means that everyone has their own timing, and their own wounds. Be prepared for different outcomes.
>
> - **What's your emotional state?**
>
>   If you're feeling too activated, angry, or vulnerable, give yourself a little more time. Practice the letter first. Say it out loud to yourself. Or talk it through with someone safe before you approach the real conversation.

Part 2: Acceptance vs. Change

Let's discuss something that lies at the heart of many people's emotional struggles, especially as we age: the tension between **acceptance** and **change**. I've seen this pattern over and over again, and maybe you've felt it yourself.

We tend to feel calm, even empowered, when we've reached one of the two ends of a spectrum. At one end, we have *acceptance*; we've made peace with what is. At the other end, we have *change*; we're actively doing something about the situation.

But there's a tricky middle zone, and it's where many people get stuck.

That space *between* acceptance and change is often where **suffering** lives. You know something's not right. Maybe a part of your life feels disappointing, or unfinished, or out of your control. But you're not ready—or don't know how—to accept it fully. At the same time, you may not feel confident, energised, or supported enough to make a change.

This *in-between* place? It's where anxiety, sadness, frustration, and helplessness tend to grow.

An Example:

Imagine someone who, after retirement, suddenly finds their days quieter than expected. The phone doesn't ring as much. They used to feel important, useful, and busy. Now they feel invisible. They're not okay with the silence, but they also don't know what to do with it. They haven't accepted it. But they also haven't found the strength or clarity to change it. And so they sit in the middle. And that's where emotional pain tends to brew—not from the silence itself, but from the disconnection between how things *are* and how we *wish* they were.

What Does It Take to Shift?

To move out of that middle zone that keeps you stuck, you need one of two things:

- A deep **letting go** and *acceptance* of what is (which takes time, reflection, and often grief)
- Or the **courage and clarity** to make a change (which takes support, energy, and sometimes some new skills)

The key is: *both are valid*. Both are powerful. And both take strength.

Acceptance is *not* giving up. **It's choosing peace over resistance.** Change is *not* denying reality. **It's believing you still have a say in it.**

And sometimes, you won't know which way to go right away. That's okay. This next exercise is here to help you explore that.

Exercise 4.2 | acceptance or change?

Take a notebook or a blank page and divide it into two sections:

Part 1: Look Back

List two to three life situations from your past that were difficult. These can be big or small.

Next to each one, write:

- Did I *accept* this, or did I *change* it?
- What helped me get to that point?
- What was difficult about it?
- How do I feel about it now?

This helps you recognise your own wisdom and strength—because you've already done this before, even if you didn't realise it.

Part 2: Look at Now

Now, write down two to three things in your current life that you struggle with or feel "stuck" in.

Next to each one, reflect on:

- Do I feel more drawn to acceptance or to change in this area?
- If I moved toward acceptance, what would I need (time, grief, permission)?
- If I moved toward change, what would I need (support, tools, courage)?
- What might be holding me back?

There's no pressure to solve it right now. This is simply to bring awareness—to shine a light into a part of yourself that might've been sitting quietly in the dark. And if it helps, here's something I often tell my clients:

Being stuck doesn't mean you're doing something wrong. It means your heart hasn't found the right door yet. And that's okay—we'll knock gently.

Part 3: Circle of Influence

There's a simple idea in psychology that has helped thousands of people feel lighter, calmer, and more in control. But like many good ideas, it's not always easy to live by. It's called the **Circle of Influence**.

Imagine two circles. One small circle in the middle—this is your *Circle of Influence*. Everything inside this circle is something you can actually **do** something about. Your thoughts. Your actions. Your reactions. The words you choose. The boundaries you set. The habits you build. The way you take care of your body. How you spend your time and energy. Your choices.

Now, outside that circle is the *Circle of Concern*. These are things that affect you or that you worry about, but that you have **little or no control** over. Other people's opinions. The past. The news. Politics. Your adult children's decisions. The way your body is ageing. Whether your neighbour learns to mind their own business. How someone treated you twenty years ago. Whether your old colleague ever apologised.

We spend *a lot* of energy in the Circle of Concern, especially when life changes, health declines, or relationships shift. It's natural. You care. You want things to be different. You wish someone had said something, done something, chosen differently.

But the more time you spend mentally circling things you *can't* control, the more helpless, frustrated, and bitter you're likely to feel. That's not weakness; that's being human.

So here's the trick:

The more energy you spend in your Circle of Influence, the **bigger** it gets.

The more energy you spend in your Circle of Concern, the **smaller** your influence starts to feel.

Focusing less on your Circle of Concern doesn't mean you stop caring about the world. It means you focus your energy where it *counts*. Where it can make a difference: in your mood, relationships, daily joy, and sense of purpose.

A few examples:

- **You can't control** whether your adult children visit as often as you'd like.
- But **you can** control how you express your needs, how you spend your alone time, and how you nurture your own connections.
- **You can't control** the fact that your body has changed.
- But **you can** decide how you move it, care for it, or speak to it.
- **You can't fix** the world or the news cycle.
- But **you can** choose your inputs, your actions, and your contribution to your own little corner of the world.

EXERCISE 4.3 | DRAWING YOUR CIRCLES

Take a blank page and draw two circles:
One small circle in the middle (label it *My Circle of Influence*)
One larger circle around it (label it *My Circle of Concern*)

Start by writing in the outer circle:

- What's been weighing on your mind lately?
- What's out of your hands?
- What's frustrating, unfair, or unresolved—but not within your control?

Now move to the inner circle:

- What *is* within your control—even if it's small?
- What can you *say, do, think,* or *focus on* differently?
- What habits or mindsets can you nurture?
- What's one action—even tiny—that you can take in the next few days?
- What do you notice about how you've been using your energy?
- What would it feel like to shift just *5% more* of your time, thoughts, and care into your circle of influence?

CHAPTER 5:
Rewriting Identity

When life shifts, when work stops, when children become adults, when health changes or loved ones pass on, it's not just the schedule that gets quiet. A deeper silence sets in. One that often carries a confronting question:

Who am I now that I am no longer who I was?

That's what this chapter is about. Identity. Not the one printed on your passport, or tied to a job title, but the inner story of who you are, what you stand for, and how you see yourself when no one else is watching.

Through my conversations, I've seen how identity becomes a particularly tender topic later in life. For decades, we have defined ourselves through what we *do*, who we *care for*, and what we *achieve*. But as those things begin to fade or change shape, it can feel as though the foundation of "you" has crumbled. It hasn't. However, it may be time to carefully and consciously reconstruct it.

We're going to do that through two key pillars:

1. The **roles** you've played (and outgrown), and
2. The **values** that have guided—and will continue to guide—you.

Let's take our time here.

Part 1: The Roles That Shape Identity

Roles are the building blocks of everyday identity. You've had many: partner, parent, grandparent, worker, caregiver, sibling, friend, leader, neighbour, fixer-of-everything. These roles give us direction and structure. They anchor us in routines and relationships. They help answer the question: *What am I needed for?*

But roles aren't permanent. Some fade with age or circumstance. Others change because the people around us change. Your children may no longer need your advice. Your profession may no longer need your expertise. A spouse may pass away, leaving the role of partner suspended in the air.

And when a role dissolves, it can feel like *you* dissolve a little too.

That feeling is deeply valid. Psychologically, when our roles shift, our identity enters a state of flux. It's like walking around in a suit that used to fit perfectly, but now pinches at the shoulders or hangs too loosely. In acceptance and commitment therapy (ACT), we often say, "You are not the role; you are the actor." You are the one who *plays* the roles. You are bigger than the script.

Letting go of a role does not erase your identity. It's an invitation to **reshape** it. In fact, each role you've ever had has left you with valuable clues about your values, your strengths, your passions. Roles are reflections. So ask yourself: *What did you enjoy being? What came naturally? What felt fulfilling?*

EXERCISE 5.1 | THE ROLES RE-IMAGINED

In your notebook, list out the major roles you've had in your life. For each one, reflect on the following questions:

- Who was I to this person or group?

- What did I contribute in that role? (Think in terms of qualities: support, humour, structure, warmth.)

- What did I love about being in this role?

- Are there parts of me from that time that I want to bring back or let go of?

- Which of my current roles do I find energising? Which feels outdated?

- How could I *update* these roles to fit who I am today?

This exercise isn't just about letting go of the past. It's about viewing your personal history as a map and using it to chart your next destination. You're still the actor. You can write new roles.

Part 2: The Values That Define You

If roles are the clothes you wear, **values** are the fabric they're made of.

Values are your inner compass. They're what make certain things feel "right" and others feel "off." They're not goals you can tick off; values are directions you keep moving toward. Love. Growth. Freedom. Kindness. Creativity. Honesty. Each person has their own unique mix.

Here's the problem: most of us don't spend time naming our values. Instead, we compare ourselves to others. We look at what other people are doing and ask, *Should I want that too?* But maybe the person you're envying is living a life aligned with *their* values, not yours. It's like being jealous of someone who runs marathons, even though you hate running.

Life—especially when we've spent decades doing what's expected of us—has a way of slowly pulling us away from our values. We follow the structure of work, family responsibilities, caregiving, and obligations. We get good at being useful. We become who others need us to be. And somewhere along the line, we forget to ask: **"What do *I* actually care about? What lights me up?"**

It's no wonder many people, especially later in life, tell me, *I don't even know what I enjoy anymore.*

That's not because something is broken. It's because you've been busy living a full life, and maybe, just maybe, it's time to reconnect with *your* direction.

Reconnecting with your values can be one of the most grounding, healing things you do at this stage. Values help you make decisions with **clarity and confidence**. They tell you where to spend your energy. They remind you who you've always been, even if that version of you has been a bit buried under all the "doing." When we live in alignment with our values, we feel fulfilled, even during challenging times. When we don't, life feels disconnected and grey.

And the beautiful part? You don't have to overhaul your whole life to start. Sometimes, it begins with one quiet question: **"What do I feel like doing today?"**

This might sound overly simple, but it's not. That little question can reawaken the voice of your values. You might realise you're craving connection. Or creativity. Or nature. Or peace. Or movement. One small action toward that feeling can shift your entire day. And with enough days, your entire sense of self.

> ### Exercise 5.2 | The daily check-in
>
> Each morning, ask yourself:
>
> - What do I feel like doing today—not what should I do, but what feels meaningful or energising?
>
> - What value might be underneath that desire (e.g., wanting to call a friend = connection, taking a walk = health or peace)?
>
> Write it down if you'd like. Even just tracking these answers over a week can show you patterns—patterns that point you toward your values in action.

Exercise 5.3 | the value check-in (expanded)

Now we go deeper. Find the worksheet on the list of values (www.chapter60.online). In your notebook, write down **six to eight values** that feel truly important to *you*. If you need help, imagine being at the end of your life, looking back: what would you be proud to have stood for?

Then, for each value, reflect:

- What does this value personally mean to me?
- How visible is this value in my life today?
- What's one way I could live this value a bit more this week?
- What tends to get in the way?

This is not about becoming a better person. It's about becoming a more you version of you. One who feels clearer, calmer, and more connected to their own life.

Part 3: Identity Lives in Memory, Too

It's easy to think identity is all about who we are *now*. But that's not the full picture. Identity isn't just made in the present; it's remembered. It lives in stories, in small moments, in old songs, in the feeling of your childhood kitchen, in the scent of your grandfather's cologne, or in the weight of a letter you once kept tucked away.

In therapy, we often say that **memory is the container of the self**. It's where we store our triumphs, our turning points, our wounds, our joy, and the tiny things that shaped us without us even realising it. And for many people later in life, there's an urge to return to these places. To look back, not to get stuck in the past, but to make sense of it. Revisiting your memories, especially the early ones, can strengthen your sense of identity now. It helps you reconnect with the traits and values you may have forgotten were yours all along. It enables you to *reclaim* parts of yourself. Especially the parts that felt the most alive.

Exercise 5.4 | the object & the emotion

Think of a meaningful object from your childhood or youth. Maybe a teddy bear, a book, a trinket, or something that sat on your bedside table.

Now ask:

- What did this object represent to me back then?
- What did I feel when I had it near me?
- Do I still long for that feeling now?
- How can I bring more of that emotion (safety, joy, connection, creativity) into my life today?

We're not just reflecting here—we're translating childhood meaning into adult nourishment.

Exercise 5.5 | the photo album conversation

Take out your old photo albums. Or a box of pictures. Or even one photo from a drawer that hasn't seen the light of day in years. Choose a few photos from different chapters of your life—childhood, teenage years, young adulthood, parenting years, work life, travels, anything that speaks to you.

Then, write or talk through these questions for each photo:

- What's happening here?
- Who am I with, and what did they mean to me?
- How old was I? What was going on in my life at the time?
- What kind of person was I back then? What traits, dreams, values did I have?
- What parts of that person still live in me?
- Is there anything I miss? Anything I want to bring forward again?

CHAPTER 5: REWRITING IDENTITY

Now here's the part I encourage you to try:

Do this with someone else. A loved one. A child. A grandchild. A neighbour. Invite them to sit with you and go through the photos. Not to be sentimental (though that's okay too), but to let them *see you*. To share your story. You'll be surprised by what memories come up when you speak them out loud.

This isn't just an exercise in memory. It's an act of identity-building. Of meaning-making. And sometimes, of connection. It turns a simple afternoon into something much more profound: a bridge between who you were, who you are, and who you're still becoming.

A message of encouragement

Your identity is not a static label. It's a living, breathing story. Shaped by what you do, what you find important, and how you remember yourself. And when life changes, your identity doesn't disappear; it just invites you to rewrite the next chapter.

Values, roles, objects from the past, and old photographs help you answer the big identity questions that often surface at this stage of life:

- *Who was I really in all those years?*
- *Who am I now?*
- *And how do I want to live the rest of my life, starting from **today**?*

Let's keep going.

CHAPTER 6:
The Courage to Change

If you've made it to this chapter, first pause and take a breath. Really. Inhale. Exhale. Let that land. You've come far. Much farther than you might even realise.

You've revisited your childhood and your earliest roles in life. You've confronted memories, regrets, and the lingering whispers of negative self-talk. You've been brave enough to ask yourself hard questions. To challenge long-held beliefs about who you are. To write letters to your past. To reflect deeply. And perhaps somewhere along the way, a little more compassion slipped in. A little more room inside you to be softer with yourself. That is one of the things that I find really important for you to start feeling.

In therapy, I often tell people that doing this kind of work—the inner kind—is one of the hardest things a person can do. It's far easier to distract ourselves, keep moving, or bury discomfort under a sense of busyness. But not you. You chose to face yourself. Not to criticise, but to understand.

This chapter is all about translating insight into movement. Action. The real-life stuff. But let's begin first with a word most people hate in therapy: **acceptance**.

I know. The moment I say it, faces twist. Eyes narrow. People sit back in their chairs and cross their arms. It's as if I'd just said, *You should give up now. Settle. Shrink yourself down and call it peace.* But that's not what real acceptance is. Not even close.

Acceptance isn't defeat. It's release.

It's the moment you stop fighting reality with clenched fists and start allowing yourself to *breathe*. It's what happens when you stop replaying that argument in your head, stop trying to rewrite the past, and say with gentleness, *It was what it was. I did what I could. And now I get to choose what's next.*

Acceptance is already a form of change. It's the kind of change that clears the fog. It softens the self-talk. It opens the door to possibility, not because you're forcing life to be different, but because you've stopped trying to control what you can't.

And that's where real movement begins, inviting in a new question: **"Given where I am now, what do I want to do with it?"**

Let's Talk About Change

Change is a tricky word at this stage of life. People assume that after a certain age, things settle. That you stop evolving. That you become who you are and stay there, fixed like cement. But you and I both know that's not true. Change doesn't belong to the young. Growth isn't owned by any generation.

Maybe, through earlier chapters, you realised you've been playing small. Or waiting. Or longing. Perhaps the roles you once had have shifted or vanished, and you're wondering what else could be out there. Perhaps you've uncovered values you hadn't thought about in decades, and now they're tugging at you.

This chapter is your invitation to *try*.

Not to overhaul your life in one weekend. Not to suddenly become someone else. But to *experiment*. To play. To take one small, shaky, courageous step forward. Let's explore how.

The Comfort Zone, the Learning Zone, and the Panic Zone

Let's picture three circles:

- The **Comfort Zone**: This is where things feel safe. You know the rules here. You can predict what will happen. But staying here too long can make it feel stale. Small. Boring.

- The **Panic Zone**: This is the other extreme. You push yourself way too far, too fast. Your nervous system freaks out. Everything feels threatening. This is not where growth happens; it's where shutdown does.

- Then there's the **Learning Zone**: The sweet spot. Slightly uncomfortable, but manageable. It's where courage meets preparation. Where new experiences can land.

Here's a psychological truth about why change feels so hard: **anxious thoughts block action**.

Your mind whispers things like:

- *What if I fail?*
- *I'll just embarrass myself.*
- *I'm too old to start now.*
- *What's the point?*

And so you don't act. You don't try. And the fear gets to win.

But when you don't try, you've already failed—100%.

When you *do* try, even just a little, the worst-case scenario rarely happens. And even if it does? Now you know you can handle it.

Most people think they have to leap from comfort straight into chaos. One of the most helpful tools I use in therapy is something called a **behavioural experiment**, and it often goes hand in hand with creating a **fear hierarchy**. The idea is simple: instead of diving headfirst into the deep end (and then never trying again because it was terrifying), you take small, manageable steps that stretch you, but don't snap you. Start with the least scary and work your way up. These small steps help you gradually challenge the anxious thoughts or avoidant behaviours that have been holding you back. It's not about doing it perfectly; it's about doing it at all.

Think of it as building a ladder toward confidence. Each rung is a task that feels just *a little* outside your comfort zone—not too easy, not too overwhelming. That sweet spot is the learning zone. At the same time, you are gathering *evidence. Was it as bad as I thought? Did I survive it? Could I do it again?* With every experiment, you start building trust in yourself, not by thinking your way out of fear, but by *acting* your way through it—gently, intentionally, and one small step at a time.

Also, keep in mind that **not every behavioural experiment will go well**. Sometimes you'll try something, and it won't land. Maybe the conversation didn't go as you hoped. Maybe the anxiety was stronger than expected. Or perhaps you backed out altogether. That's okay. It's not a test you pass or fail; it's a tool to gather information. You're training your mind and body to tolerate more discomfort. This method turns abstract goals into lived experiences, and that's when change becomes real.

Exercise 6.1 | build your fear ladder

Let's say you discovered something throughout this book. That you want to travel more. Or start a creative project. Or be more assertive. Or maybe even finally tell your adult child how you *really* feel. Maybe you want to set boundaries or try something you've put off for decades.

How to build it:

1. **Name your goal** (e.g., "I want to be more assertive.")
2. Write down all the situations related to this that make you feel nervous or unsure.
3. Rank them from least anxiety-provoking to most.
4. Start with the easiest one.

Example: *Becoming more assertive*

- Practice saying "no" out loud to myself in the mirror.
- Call someone instead of sending a message to say "no."
- Tell a friend honestly how I felt about a past situation.
- Set a boundary with a family member.
- Ask someone for help when I usually wouldn't.

Exercise 6.2 | the behaviour experiment

Now you can choose one situation on the fear ladder that makes you anxious and design an experiment to *test* those fears. You can also use the worksheet (www.chapter60.online).

Step 1: Identify the Belief

Write down the belief you're going to test.

If I say no to my friend when they ask for something, they will be angry or stop liking me.

Step 2: Rate Your Belief Strength

On a scale from 0 to 100%, how strongly do you believe this?

Step 3: Design the Experiment

Think of a small, low-risk situation where you can practice.

Example Experiment:

The next time my friend asks me to do something I don't want to do—like meeting up when I'm tired—I will politely say, "I can't today, but I hope you have a good time."

Step 4: Make a Prediction

What do you predict will happen?

I think my friend will be disappointed and might stop asking me to do things with them.

Step 5: Carry Out the Experiment

Go ahead and do the action. Write down exactly what happened.

Step 6: Reflect

Did what you predicted happen?

How did the person actually respond?

How did you feel afterwards?

Step 7: Update the Belief

Based on the outcome, would you adjust your belief? What would you say to yourself next time?

PART TWO:
The Realities of Later Life

FELICIA ZEVEN

CHAPTER SIXTY+

———— ◦⊙◦ ————

As we've explored in the first part of this book, personal growth, emotional insight, and meaningful change are still deeply possible at any age. But with age also come unique realities; themes that may not have been as pressing in earlier years, but now shape your everyday life, your relationships, and your sense of self. This part of the book is dedicated to those themes. They often arise in therapy, and they deserve attention, care, and honest reflection.

You may notice that my tone shifts slightly in the following chapters. It's no longer quite the same as sitting with me in a therapy session. Instead, I write more from a place of comfort and recognition, as if offering consoling words rather than direct guidance. Not to create distance, but to honour the sensitive nature of these experiences. I want you to feel seen in what you're facing, to know that these topics are real, often spoken about, and treated with deep respect.

These coming chapters are not simply about *solving problems.* They are about understanding the deeper layers of what it means to grow older in a world that often looks away from ageing. Whether you're dealing with loss, physical change, retirement, or questions of meaning, my goal remains the same: to meet you with clarity, depth, and compassion. The following chapters cover the most common themes that I discuss with my clients in therapy.

CHAPTER 7:
Loss and Grief—Living with What Can't Be Fixed

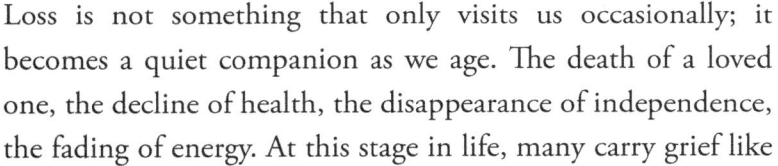

Loss is not something that only visits us occasionally; it becomes a quiet companion as we age. The death of a loved one, the decline of health, the disappearance of independence, the fading of energy. At this stage in life, many carry grief like a second skin. And while society often makes you feel that you should be "used to it by now," grief does not respect timelines.

There's the sharp grief, the one that arrives like a wave and knocks you over when someone you love dies. And then there's the slow grief—the one that lingers and whispers in the background, a sense of absence that appears during dinner, holidays, or quiet Sunday mornings.

Grieving isn't about forgetting. Nor is it about moving on. It's about learning *how to live* with the absence. The loss of a partner, a sibling, a dear friend doesn't just leave a hole in your heart; it can unsettle your sense of self. If you've spent decades in a particular role (spouse, caregiver, daughter, companion), then grief can make you feel like you've lost yourself along with the person. You might find yourself wondering, *Who am I now?* Not as a rhetorical question, but as an honest inquiry. Let this be a time of rediscovery; not to replace anyone, but to recognise that your identity continues to evolve.

For some, life after loss feels *directionless*. Every day, decisions that used to be shared now rest on your shoulders. Some clients describe it as a fog they can't quite lift. Others find they spend every minute of the day thinking about the person they've lost, replaying memories, or regretting things left unsaid.

Regret is an everyday companion to grief. You might wish you'd asked more questions, been more patient, or expressed love more often. These thoughts can feel painful, even unbearable, but they are also a sign of the deep bond you shared. With time, regret can become reflection, and reflection can open the door to healing.

Complicated Grief

While grief has no fixed timeline, sometimes it can become what professionals call a "complicated" or "prolonged grief disorder." This happens when the grieving process remains stuck; even after many months or years, the pain feels just as raw, your daily functioning is severely impaired, and your life feels as though it has stopped moving forward.

In such cases, people may:

- Avoid anything that reminds them of their loss
- Feel intense anger, guilt, or numbness
- Lose interest in activities or relationships they once valued
- Experience persistent longing or disbelief

If you recognise yourself in this, know that you are not broken. You may need more psychological support, time, and space to process your grief more fully.

When Grief Changes Everything

Some people are left not only with emotional pain but with a complete disruption of everyday life. In many couples, one partner may have been responsible for managing the bills, appointments, driving, or social planning. After their loss, the surviving partner may feel unequipped, even helpless. It's not weakness; it's reality. Grieving, while simultaneously learning a new way of living, is incredibly demanding.

If you feel overwhelmed by daily life, start with small, doable steps:

- Make a list of what feels hardest right now
- Ask someone you trust to help with just one of those items

- Choose one new thing to learn each week (e.g., online banking, cooking, scheduling)

Your confidence will grow with time, even if it doesn't feel like it now.

Different People, Different Grief

It's also important to know that **no two people grieve the same way**. When parents lose a child or grandchild, for example, it's not uncommon for each partner to express their grief differently. One may need to talk constantly, while the other prefers silence. One person may cling to memories, while the other may avoid them. This mismatch can cause tension and misunderstanding.

If you're grieving alongside someone else, try to:

- Respect each other's process
- Avoid judging what the other "should" be feeling
- Make space for both shared and private mourning

The Emotions of Grief

Grief can manifest in many forms: sadness, anger, numbness, anxiety, relief (especially after a long illness), guilt, or even laughter at unexpected moments. These aren't contradictions; they're all valid parts of grieving.

You might feel angry at your loved one for leaving, at the world for continuing as if nothing happened, or at yourself for not doing things differently. Let that anger speak. Write it down. Yell into a pillow. Give it space without shame.

You might also feel nothing at all. A hollow emptiness. That doesn't mean you didn't love them; it just means your system is trying to protect you from overwhelm. Numbness is a kind of armour, and even that is part of the healing process.

The Stages of Mourning

You may have heard of the five stages of grief: **denial**, **anger**, **bargaining**, **depression**, and **acceptance**. These aren't steps you climb in a neat order. They come and go. You may feel acceptance one morning, and crushing sadness that same afternoon.

Think of these stages not as rules, but as common emotional experiences:

- **Denial:** *This can't be real.*
- **Anger:** *Why did this happen? Who's to blame?*
- **Bargaining:** *If only I had . . . Maybe I should have . . .*
- **Depression:** *This hurts more than I imagined.*
- **Acceptance:** *This is my reality now, and I'm learning how to live with it.*

You may revisit any of these again and again. That's normal. Grief is not a problem to be solved. It's a companion to be acknowledged. You carry it because you loved. And over time, even though the pain may never disappear entirely, your life can grow around the loss. Let grief walk beside you, but don't let it silence you.

What Can You Do?

- **Acknowledge your loss.** Say it out loud. Name what is gone. Let it be real.

- **Give yourself permission to grieve in your own way.** There's no single correct method.

- **Identify what still remains.** What brings even a sliver of meaning, comfort, or hope?

- **Don't isolate yourself.** Grief can feel lonely, but connection helps.

- **Get support.** Friends, family, or professional counsellors can offer a lifeline.

Exercise 7.1 | Write a letter to the person you've lost

Write a letter to the person you are grieving. Tell them what they meant to you, what you miss, what you've learned. Let the words flow freely.

Keep it, burn it, or read it to someone you trust. The act of writing can make space for healing.

CHAPTER 8:
Retirement—When the Alarm Clock Stops

Retirement. The word alone holds so much weight. For decades, it might have shimmered in the distance like a long-awaited destination—a promise of freedom after years of early mornings, deadlines, and responsibilities. Perhaps you imagined it as a peaceful horizon filled with long holidays, time with grandchildren, gardening, painting, or simply not having to rush anywhere ever again.

And for many people, it *is* that. Some clients I meet are absolutely thriving in their retirement; waking up slowly with coffee and a book, rediscovering their creativity, or throwing themselves into volunteer work with more passion than they ever had in their professional careers. For them, retirement is not an ending but a long-awaited beginning.

But not everyone feels that way.

Some people arrive in retirement and feel . . . *adrift*. There's no alarm clock to hate, but also no reason to get up. The schedule is gone. The deadlines vanish, and sometimes so does the sense of direction. There are no meetings, no calls, no colleagues who expect your input: no patients, no clients, no classes to teach or projects to deliver. You may find yourself asking quietly, "And now what?"

We tend to forget that work is more than just a way to pay the bills. For many of us, it offers **structure**, **purpose**, and **identity**. You weren't just *doing* a job; you *were* someone in that role. You were the teacher who made children feel seen, the nurse who calmed anxious patients, the office manager who kept everything running, the shopkeeper who knew every customer's name. So when work ends, it's not just the job that disappears. A part of your identity retires too. I often hear people say things like:

I was always the one people came to for help. Now, I feel invisible.

I knew who I was at work. Now, I don't know what to say when people ask what I do.

These are not just passing thoughts; they reflect a deeper emotional process. What you're experiencing may resemble grief. And grief isn't just about losing someone; it's about losing a version of yourself, a rhythm of life, a sense of being needed.

Another common experience is the **vacuum of time**. It's not just that you have more of it—it's that the structure that used to give shape to your days has disappeared. This lack of external rhythm can feel disorienting. Some people become restless, some even depressed. Time begins to lose definition. It stretches endlessly, or it blurs.

When you pair that with other possible stressors, such as financial worries, health issues, loneliness, or a partner who has a very different idea of what retirement should look like, you're suddenly dealing with a perfect storm of emotional challenges.

It's important to say this clearly: **these feelings are valid**. You're not being ungrateful. You're not doing retirement *wrong*. You are adjusting to a life transition as significant—and as emotionally complex—as starting your first job, having your first child, or moving to a new country.

But there is one thing to keep in mind: while these feelings are normal, **they need care**. Left unchecked, they can pull you into passivity or hopelessness. They can rob you of your energy, your self-worth, and your will to shape this next chapter with intention.

Gently Rebuilding Rhythm, Meaning, and Joy

What I often encourage clients to do is **not to rush**, but also **not to freeze**. You don't need to have it all figured out. But small steps matter. Think of this new phase as a blank canvas—intimidating, yes, but also full of potential. You don't have to paint a masterpiece today. But you can pick a colour. Make a mark.

Start by introducing three types of activities back into your week: those that give you **pleasure**, those that give you a **sense of purpose**, and those that **challenge** you in some way. This blend keeps your mind engaged, your body active, and your spirit connected to something meaningful.

One thing I've noticed in my work is that retirement can act like a magnifying glass. Whatever patterns you had before, whether it's how you handled stress, how you nurtured relationships, or how you took care of yourself, they become more visible when the busy distractions of working life fall away. If you tend to overwork and neglect friendships, the quiet might suddenly feel lonely. If you relied heavily on routine, the open space might feel unsettling. This is not a flaw; it's information. It's an opportunity to notice what's been missing and to choose, perhaps for the first time in decades, what you want your days to look like.

It's also worth acknowledging that some people discover they've been living parallel lives with their partner, meeting at the end of the day and sharing weekends, each with their own separate roles. Retirement suddenly puts you together in the same space far more than before. For some couples, it's delightful; for others, it can feel like a collision. This doesn't mean your relationship is failing. It means you're entering a new phase that may require renegotiation, specifically regarding space, expectations, and how to balance shared time with personal time.

Then there's the subtle but powerful shift in how the world sees you. Our culture has a tendency to equate worth with productivity, which means retirement can feel like stepping out of the spotlight and into the shadows. But remember: value isn't measured by how many hours you clock. The knowledge you've gained, the perspective you carry, the empathy you've cultivated—they don't expire with your last payslip. You may have to be the one to remind yourself (and sometimes others) of that truth.

One of the most liberating things about this stage is that you have more freedom to align your days with your own values rather than someone else's schedule. That doesn't mean every moment will be filled with joy or purpose . . . no stage of life works that way. But it does mean you can start experimenting. Maybe you try something you never had time for before: a pottery class, joining a choir, mentoring a young person in your old profession, or finally writing that story you've been carrying in your head for decades.

If the idea of *reinventing yourself* feels too big or exhausting, then don't reinvent. Just evolve. Keep what still fits, let go of what doesn't, and allow yourself to be curious about what might be next. Retirement isn't a single decision; it's a process. It unfolds over months and years, changing as you do. Some days will feel light and open, while others may feel aimless or heavy. Both are normal. The important thing is to stay in motion, not rushing, not forcing, but gently leaning toward the things that make you feel alive.

Exercise 8.1 | Types of activities

- **Joy:**

    What lifts your spirit, even a little? Maybe it's music, walking in nature, baking, watching birds, playing with a grandchild, or dancing in the living room.

- **Purpose:**

    What gives you a sense of meaning or usefulness? This could be mentoring someone, helping a neighbour, working on a creative project, or volunteering once a month.

- **Connection:**

    What brings you into contact with others? A phone call, a shared coffee, a class, a choir, a club . . . or just chatting with someone at the market.

Start small. **One thing from each category per week.** Let that be your gentle rhythm. You'll be surprised how even a little structure can restore a sense of being alive, rather than just "retired." And remember: there is no right way to retire. Only your way. Be kind to yourself. Moving from *I must* to *I may* is a freedom that requires a new kind of courage—and you have more of that than you think.

CHAPTER 9:
Loneliness—And Why It Hurts So Much

Let me share something with you from the therapy room.

When I meet new clients for the first time, I go through a standard checklist. It's part of the intake process, specifically questions about mood, energy, sleep, appetite, and anxiety. I'll ask: *Have you been feeling down? Any panic attacks? Trouble concentrating?* Sometimes, people shake their heads and say, *No, I'm fine, really.*

But then we come to one quiet question—one that isn't shouted as loudly as depression or anxiety—and I ask gently: *Do you ever feel lonely?*

That's often the moment when something shifts in the room. A pause. A sigh. And sometimes, unexpectedly, tears. Not because the person didn't know they were lonely, but because they hadn't said it out loud in a long time—maybe ever.

They tell me:

I don't know what I'm here for anymore.
My children are busy with their own lives.
People just kind of . . . faded.
I'm surrounded by others sometimes, but I feel invisible.

Loneliness is powerful. And it's painful. But perhaps most of all, it's *human*.

Loneliness is not just the absence of people around you. You can feel it while scrolling through messages. While laughing with a group of friends. While sitting next to your partner of forty years. Loneliness isn't just about being alone. It's about feeling unseen, disconnected, or no longer *needed* in the way you once were.

And here's the truth that often surprises people: **loneliness can be physically painful**. Brain imaging studies show that loneliness activates the same brain regions as physical pain. It's not *just in your head* . . . your body feels it too.

Why? Because connection is not a luxury. It's a biological need. We are social creatures, **wired for attachment**. For touch, for laughter, for being remembered. Without enough of those things, our nervous system interprets it as a threat. And slowly, it starts to affect everything: mood, memory, motivation, even immunity.

In therapy, I often see how loneliness creeps in slowly. It's not always dramatic. It happens over time.

- Your children grow up. Their lives are whole. You love them deeply, but sometimes it feels like you've been shelved.

- Friends move away. Others become less mobile. Some pass away.

- You used to meet people at work or during your children's school years. That routine is gone now.

- Health issues might make it harder to leave the house or join in.

- Or maybe you were always more introverted, and now the world feels harder to reach.

And because the change is gradual, many people don't realise how lonely they are until the emptiness is impossible to ignore. The days stretch long. The silence becomes loud. And a creeping question settles in: *What's the point of me now?*

Loneliness and Meaninglessness: A Close Relationship

One of the lesser-talked-about side effects of chronic loneliness is **a loss of meaning**. We will cover this more in-depth in Chapter 12.

When no one seems to need you, ask for your advice, or share their daily life with you, it's easy to feel like your presence no longer matters. And when that feeling sticks around, it can lead to hopelessness. That's why loneliness is so closely linked to depression in older adults.

Throughout most of our lives, connection is woven into our daily roles and routines: parenting, working, caregiving, and community involvement. These roles give us proximity and a sense of purpose.

When they shift or disappear, the scaffolding of social life can quietly collapse. It's not that you became less valuable. It's that the *structures* that carried the connection are no longer in place. And unless we intentionally build new ones, loneliness fills the space.

And this is important: loneliness can feed **shame**. It whispers, *You're too old to make new friends* or *No one is thinking of you*. I hear these sentences often during my sessions. And I say clearly: *They are lies*. But they can feel genuine. And if you believe them, they keep you from reaching out, which in turn makes loneliness worse. It's a vicious cycle. And breaking it starts with knowing: **you're not alone in feeling alone**. You are still capable of connection. You are still someone worth knowing, worth listening to, and worth missing. You don't have to rebuild your entire social world. Just soften one wall. Open one window.

And here's another truth worth remembering: loneliness is not a permanent label; it's a current state. Feelings—even the heavy ones—shift when we introduce new experiences. Sometimes the first step is not to find "new best friends," but to simply place yourself where human life is happening: at a café, a community garden, a local library event. You don't need to speak to anyone at first; even being among the gentle hum of other people can help reawaken that sense of belonging.

There's also a kind of loneliness that comes not from a lack of people, but from a lack of *emotional closeness*. Family might surround you, yet you feel that no one truly *knows* you anymore. That's why it can be so powerful to reconnect with one person from your past, or to find someone new who shares your particular interests or humour. Meaningful connection is about quality, not quantity.

It's worth noting that our brains remain capable of forming new bonds well into our later years. Neuroplasticity doesn't vanish at sixty-five. The circuits that light up when we feel understood, valued, and included can still be activated. And the more often they are, the more resilient your mind and mood become.

EXERCISE 9.1 | THE CIRCLES OF CONNECTION

Draw three circles like a target:

- In the **inner circle**, write the people you feel closest to.
- In the **middle circle**, those you like but don't see often.
- In the **outer circle**, acquaintances—like the friendly man at the market, or your old neighbour.

Now ask yourself:

- Who gives me energy?
- Who would I like to bring a little closer?
- What qualities or attributes does this person bring out in me?
- What's one gentle thing I could do this week to reach out?

CHAPTER 10:
This Body, Now—When Physical Changes Shake the Ground Beneath You

There is a moment when the body no longer keeps pace with the mind. You may still feel curious, sharp, and eager inside, but your knees say no. Your stamina dwindles. A familiar street now feels longer than it used to. And suddenly, what was once automatic—running up the stairs, reading a menu without glasses, hopping on your bike—begins to require effort, planning, or help.

That shift can *shake* you.

Physical decline, whether slow and steady or abrupt through a health crisis, doesn't just affect your body. It touches something much deeper: your identity, your sense of freedom, your plans for the future, and even your place in the world. These changes can bring waves of fear, insecurity, or grief. They confront you with realities you might have preferred to delay or deny: *What will I still be able to do? Will I become dependent? What will happen if I can't manage on my own?*

For some, these questions come into sharp focus after a sudden medical event: perhaps a stroke, a heart attack, or another health scare that arrived unexpectedly. If that's happened to you, then you know the jolt it delivers. One day, your body is familiar, capable, and taken for granted, and the next, it's foreign, fragile, unpredictable. That kind of shock can shatter your trust in your own physical self. It's not just recovery from the event that matters, but also the slow, often invisible task of rebuilding your sense of safety within your own skin.

In therapy, we often speak about the *emotional recovery* that follows physical trauma. There may be fear in every strange sensation, anxiety about recurrence, or a subtle retreat from life—avoiding things you once enjoyed because they now feel risky. And yet, many people also describe these events as *turning points*. Moments that cracked life open. That reordered priorities. That made clear what truly matters and what doesn't.

You might find yourself asking bigger questions after such a shock: *What do I want to do with the time I have? Who do I want to be close to? What am I no longer willing to postpone?* These are important, tender questions not just about survival, but about how to live meaningfully, even in a body that has changed. If you're still recovering from a serious illness or health scare, be gentle with yourself. Rebuilding trust in your body takes time. It's not about returning to who you were before, but about learning who you are now and what this version of you still wants and needs from life.

The Mental Weight of Physical Limitations

Physical limitations mean not only less movement—they also mean a greater mental load. Every trip outside the house might now require a calculation: *Is there parking nearby? Are there too many stairs? Will I be able to keep up?* You might find yourself opting out of invitations not because you don't want to go, but because you're afraid you won't be able to manage.

This fear is real and valid. Many clients describe how a single fall or diagnosis made them suddenly hyper-aware of their fragility. Their world shrinks a little. And with each shrinking, their mood and sense of self-worth can begin to follow. It's not just the pain or fatigue; it's the slow erosion of spontaneity, of ease.

Fear can easily spiral into avoidance. Maybe you stop going to the market on your own. Or skip social gatherings. Perhaps you postpone that visit to your child or put off seeing a friend. Fear says: *What if I fall, get sick, need the bathroom, or simply can't keep up?* Before long, the fear becomes more *disabling* than the physical limitation itself.

For many, ageing brings difficult decisions. The house that once felt warm and safe may now be full of stairs, tripping hazards, or long distances from care. Maybe it's time to move to a place with an elevator, or a town with better healthcare. These changes can feel like surrendering a part of your life story. A loss of independence. Some clients tell me how painful it is to pack up decades of memories. Others wrestle with guilt, especially if the move was triggered by their needs and their partner or family had to adapt.

Health issues often come with another layer of tension: *the looming future*. Perhaps you're caring for a partner who is ill. Or you notice your own body faltering more than theirs. Suddenly, moments of quiet togetherness bring an underlying ache. The question no one wants to voice: *What happens to me if something happens to you?*

This fear is both profoundly human and incredibly heavy. For couples, it can create emotional distance or a sense of clinging. For individuals, it may lead to excessive worrying about wills, funeral arrangements, or emergency contacts. These thoughts, while normal, can become overwhelming if they start to dominate daily life.

And this is where a quiet shift often begins internally.

As physical health changes, a more introspective, often tender conversation with yourself begins. You may grieve the younger, healthier version of yourself. You may feel betrayed by your body, feeling angry that it no longer functions the way it used to. Or you might feel shame for needing help, for no longer being the one who *provides* but instead the one who must now *receive*.

But here's an important truth: **your body isn't your enemy**. It's doing its best: it's adapting, recalibrating, holding you up in new ways. Ageing and illness are not personal failures; they are part of being human. In therapy, we often try to soften the inner dialogue. Instead of saying, *I can't do anything anymore*, we gently ask: *What can I still do?* We practise holding space for grief without letting it define the whole story.

What's more, your partner or children may also be navigating their own emotions, such as fear, helplessness, impatience, or guilt. These changes can test relationships in quiet, complicated ways. You might feel like a burden, even if your loved ones don't see you that way. In response, you might withdraw, become irritable, or struggle to ask for what you need.

And yet, they can also open up space for something else: honesty. A deeper kind of presence. When you can say to a loved one, *I'm scared* or *I miss how things used to be*, you make room for authentic connection, not despite the changes, but *because* of them. The key is open conversation: acknowledging that things are different, but also affirming the love, the humour, and the connection that remain. Doing so can serve as an opportunity to deepen intimacy, even as you mourn what's been lost.

> ### Exercise 10.1 | A timeline of strength
>
> Draw a timeline of your life, decade by decade. In each, write down one thing your body allowed you to do that you're grateful for.
>
> Then, in this current chapter, write down what your body still lets you experience—even if it's small. Breathing in fresh air. Laughing. Cooking a meal. Holding a grandchild.
>
> **Let it remind you:** your body has always been your companion. It has changed, but it hasn't abandoned you.

Exercise 10.2 | how to re-build trust with your body

You don't need to love your body in order to treat it well. You don't need to feel strong in order to take the next step. You just need to begin a new kind of relationship with your body, one built not on performance, but on partnership.

Here's how you can start:

1. **Ask New Questions**

   - What does my body need more of right now (rest, gentleness, hydration, movement)?
   - What can I still do that brings me joy or comfort?
   - Where can I safely push my edge without fear of taking the wheel?

2. **Change the Narrative**

Instead of *I can't do anything anymore*, try:

   - "I do things differently now"
   - "I'm adapting"
   - "I'm learning to work with my body, not against it"

3. **Create Small Rituals of Respect**

    - Moisturize your skin slowly.

    - Stretch each morning, even for five minutes.

    - Wear clothes that feel good—not just functional.

    - Celebrate small wins: "I walked to the mailbox today. That matters."

CHAPTER 11:
Bridging the Generational Gap

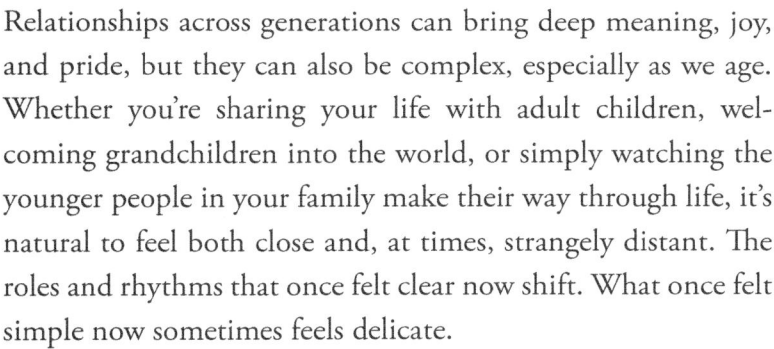

Relationships across generations can bring deep meaning, joy, and pride, but they can also be complex, especially as we age. Whether you're sharing your life with adult children, welcoming grandchildren into the world, or simply watching the younger people in your family make their way through life, it's natural to feel both close and, at times, strangely distant. The roles and rhythms that once felt clear now shift. What once felt simple now sometimes feels delicate.

Perhaps you find yourself navigating unfamiliar territory: wanting to stay close to your adult children without seeming intrusive or caring for grandchildren while also beginning to need care yourself. Perhaps you feel proud of your children's independence, but also feel left out and uncertain about where you fit. Or you long for a deeper connection, but don't quite know how to ask for it. These are not signs of failure. They're signs of change. And they are more common than you might think.

As we age, one of the most emotionally challenging transitions is watching the roles within our family quietly *rearrange* themselves. If you were once the one your children leaned on for advice, support, or direction, it can be disorienting when they begin to guide you instead. You might find them offering unsolicited advice about your health, your finances, or how you spend your time. Even when this is done with good intentions, it can sometimes evoke unexpected emotions, such as pride, resistance, frustration, or even shame.

Psychologically, when we lose some degree of autonomy or authority, it can trigger a sense of identity loss. You may ask yourself quietly: *What is my place in this family if I'm no longer needed in the same way?*

Research into ageing and family dynamics confirms that these transitions, especially when not openly discussed, can lead to internal confusion and interpersonal tension. You begin to feel like you're walking on eggshells, trying not to say too much, not to do too little. It's a kind of invisible grief: grieving the closeness you once had, the certainty of your role, the ease of communication.

One of the most painful misconceptions about ageing is the notion that relinquishing control means relinquishing love. But they are not the same. You may not be steering the ship anymore, but you are still profoundly needed—as an emotional anchor, a wise observer, a source of continuity.

Your children might make decisions you wouldn't. Your grandchildren might seem consumed by their phones or uninterested in your stories. That can hurt. But love doesn't mean agreement. And closeness doesn't always look the same as it used to.

Over time, the most enduring relationships are those that adapt and evolve. Rather than holding on tightly to the way things used to be, it helps to ask: *How can I show love in the way they are most able to receive it?* This might mean offering advice only when asked, respecting choices you don't fully understand, or accepting that being part of someone's life today sometimes means being on the periphery: cheering from the sidelines instead of standing at the centre.

Boundaries That Protect Love, Instead of Pushing It Away

Sometimes, you may find yourself in the position of giving more than you had planned: babysitting grandchildren several days a week, stepping in to help with your adult children's financial stress, or being the one they turn to when their own lives feel chaotic. While it can feel good to be needed, over time, this dynamic can become unbalanced. And often, the people we love most are also the ones with whom setting boundaries feels hardest. You may feel torn between wanting to help and knowing that your energy is more limited than it once was. Perhaps you say yes when you're tired, or agree to things out of guilt, only to feel quietly resentful afterward. This inner tension is not selfishness. It's your mind and body trying to tell you something important: *that your limits matter, too.*

Setting boundaries with family, especially with younger generations, is often an act of care and consideration, not only for yourself, but for the relationship itself. When we ignore our own needs repeatedly, we often end up withdrawing emotionally or offering help with a silent undercurrent of resentment. And over time, this erodes the connection. Boundaries, when set with warmth and clarity, allow relationships to breathe. They say, *I care about you, and I also need to care for myself.* Intergenerational relationships are constantly evolving. They require patience, flexibility, and a willingness to let go of the idea that love must always look the same. You don't have to be the all-knowing parent anymore. And you don't have to be the endlessly available grandparent either.

Unspoken Wounds:
Coping with Distance in Close Relationships

Not all family relationships follow the script we imagined. Some are filled with warmth and mutual care, while others carry layers of tension, misunderstanding, or silence that stretch across years. As we grow older, unresolved issues within families—especially those involving adult children or siblings—can come into sharper focus. Perhaps a child no longer speaks to you. Perhaps there's a pattern of conflict, or a quiet, aching distance that no one knows how to bridge. These kinds of disconnections can feel like an invisible wound: not always seen from the outside, but felt deeply within.

Family estrangement is more common than most people discuss, and yet, when it occurs, it can feel profoundly isolating. You may wrestle with questions that have no easy answers:

CHAPTER 11: BRIDGING THE GENERATIONAL GAP

Where did things go wrong? Should I reach out again? Was it something I did? Why don't they want me in their lives? These thoughts often loop in the mind and can stir up guilt, shame, anger, or heartbreak, especially if you feel like your intentions were misunderstood or your efforts unrecognised.

I often see how unresolved family tensions can lead to a chronic kind of grief. This isn't the grief of death, but the grief of a relationship that still exists in name or memory, but not in connection. It can be just as painful. And unlike death, it lacks the clear rituals of mourning or the social permission to speak openly about the loss. If this is your experience, here are some truths I want you to hold on to:

You are allowed to grieve the family you hoped for, the one you tried to build, the one you perhaps still long for. Grief doesn't mean giving up; it means honouring what mattered and what still hurts.

You are not responsible for carrying all the weight of the relationship. Families are systems, and no rupture is ever caused or healed by just one person. Sometimes the stories we carry about "being the fixer" keep us stuck in a cycle of blame or silence. At a certain point, peace comes from letting go of what we cannot control, including how others respond or choose to live their lives.

You are also allowed to protect yourself. If communication with a family member brings more pain than healing—if it constantly reopens old wounds—you're not required to keep sacrificing your emotional well-being for the sake of appearances.

Boundaries can be acts of love, too: for yourself, and for what you've already endured.

And finally, you can still find and offer love. When traditional family ties are strained or broken, you can make room for chosen family: friends, neighbours, community members, or even younger people who look up to you in quiet ways. These relationships may not replace the ones you've lost, but they can remind you that your story isn't over. Connection is still possible. And you are still worthy of being seen, heard, and valued.

Exercise 11.1 | The "Two-way" letter

Choose one person from a younger generation you care about: a child, grandchild, niece, or even a neighbour. Write them a letter in two parts.

Part 1: What do you admire about them? What do you hope they know about you? What memories do you cherish together?

Part 2: What are your hopes for your relationship now? Is there something you'd like to ask, share, or understand better?

You don't need to send it. However, writing the letter can help clarify your feelings, boundaries, and love.

CHAPTER 12:
The Meaning of Life— A Conversation Worth Having

This chapter almost didn't make it into the book.

Not because it isn't essential; on the contrary, it might be the most important one of all. But it's a topic that many people, including psychologists like myself, find difficult to approach. It's abstract, elusive, and doesn't come with simple answers or neat checklists. Still, I kept hearing it in my therapy sessions, not always in direct words, but in the pauses, the tears, the quiet confessions:

I just don't see the point anymore.
What's it all been for?
Does any of this still matter?

That's why this final chapter exists. It's here for the conversations that usually happen in whispers, if they happen at all. And it's especially here for those in the second half of life, when the question of meaning often returns louder, heavier, and more personal than ever before.

Why This Question Emerges Now

When we're young, meaning often feels obvious. You raise children. You build a career. You strive for goals, for connection, for stability. But in the later decades of life, things shift. Children may have grown distant, careers are behind you, roles have changed, and the busyness that once filled your calendar might now be replaced with long hours of reflection.

In therapy, clients often begin asking questions they'd pushed aside for years:
What legacy do I leave behind?
Who am I now that I'm not working?
What makes my life meaningful when I don't feel needed the same way anymore?

These are deeply human questions. And they don't come with clear answers. What makes them more difficult is that some people reach this point and realise they don't feel much meaning at all. That realisation can lead to despair or hopelessness, especially if physical health is declining, social connections have become thinner, or one's days feel repetitive and isolated.

But meaning doesn't disappear with age. It simply asks to be approached differently.

CHAPTER 12: THE MEANING OF LIFE—A CONVERSATION WORTH HAVING

What Psychologists Understand About Meaning

Psychiatrist and writer Irvin Yalom, who has spent a lifetime exploring existential concerns, described **meaninglessness** as one of the four core existential anxieties (alongside *death*, *freedom*, and *isolation*). He acknowledged that meaning isn't something we stumble upon by accident; it's something we create. For Yalom, the unsettling truth is that life offers no inherent blueprint. There is no cosmic script to follow, no preordained set of instructions that tells us who to be or what to value. This recognition can create a deep sense of disorientation, as though the solid ground beneath us has dissolved. Yet Yalom views this confrontation not as a pathology to be eradicated but as an invitation to take responsibility for authorship of one's own life. When we acknowledge that no one else can hand us meaning, we also discover the liberating possibility of shaping it ourselves. The work, from this view, is to *tolerate the discomfort of uncertainty* long enough to explore what truly matters, to speak openly about our sense of emptiness without rushing to fill it with distractions, and to weave together a personal framework of significance that reflects our own choices rather than inherited scripts.

This is where *logotherapy*, the approach developed by neurologist and psychologist Viktor Frankl, can offer direction. Frankl proposed that meaning isn't found by chasing happiness or success, but by finding purpose in small, grounded ways— through acts of love, moments of connection, *contributions to others*, and even in *how we respond to adversity*. For Frankl, even suffering can hold meaning if we choose to react to it with courage, integrity, or compassion. This approach reframes the search for meaning as an active process: rather than asking what the overall purpose of life is, we ask, *What is life asking of me right now?* In this way, the overwhelming scale of "finding meaning" becomes manageable, grounded in small but intentional actions: a kind word to a stranger, the persistence to complete a creative project, the patience to nurture a garden, the resolve to get up again after a day that went badly.

When these two perspectives are brought together, they create a kind of double movement. Yalom encourages us to confront the stark reality that meaninglessness is an inherent part of the human condition and that it will never entirely disappear. In doing so, we free ourselves from the illusion that there is some external, definitive answer waiting to be uncovered. Frankl then offers a practical path forward, showing that even within this uncertainty, we can commit to purposeful acts that anchor our lives in significance.

Finding Meaning in the Midst of Change

As we grow older, our sense of meaning often shifts away from "achievement" and more toward **presence**, **wisdom**, and **connection**. This can be beautiful, but it can also feel destabilising if your sense of purpose was long tied to productivity or being needed.

Many of my clients experience this transition as a kind of grief. They grieve their younger bodies, their busier schedules, their sharper memories. They wonder:

If I'm no longer doing all the things I used to, what value do I bring?

One client, a retired doctor, put it plainly: *I used to save lives. Now I don't have anything left to offer.* In our sessions, we explored how his knowledge, kindness, and presence were still making a difference in the world, though perhaps in quieter, less visible ways.

Another woman, who had spent years caring for her family, now faced an empty house and an unfamiliar silence. Through therapy, she began to find meaning in mentoring young mothers at a local community centre. She said: *Turns out, I have decades of experience to pass on.*

Meaning Doesn't Always Feel Good

This is an important point: **meaning and happiness are not the same**. A meaningful life isn't one without pain. In fact, some of the most meaningful chapters of our lives can be full of hardship. What gives our lives depth is often the way we navigate those challenging chapters—the way we love through illness, the way we show up for others, the way we reflect, grow, and forgive. The small moments where we choose to keep going when we could have shut down. These are acts of meaning, even when they don't feel triumphant.

> ### Exercise 12.1 | Meaning mapping
>
> Take a quiet moment. Reflect on the following three questions and jot down whatever comes up. Don't edit or overthink:
>
> - **What moments in your life have felt the most meaningful?**
> - **Who or what gives your life a sense of purpose now?**
> - **What small act could you do this week that would feel purposeful, even just a little?**

Often, meaning doesn't arrive as a sudden revelation; it accumulates. It grows through tiny decisions over time. Your meaning may not be what it was ten years ago. It may not be what it will be in ten years. That's not a failure. That's part of being human.

And if you feel lost in this moment, unsure of your meaning, that's okay too. This chapter is not to pressure you into finding answers, but to let you know you are **allowed to ask the question**. You are permitted to be searching. You are allowed to sit with the discomfort of not knowing. Sometimes, just naming the question brings clarity. The meaning of your life isn't behind you. It's not only in the big moments, or in the years when you were most active or needed. It's also here in this exact season. In how you speak, how you care, how you reflect, and how you choose to spend your remaining time.

You are still becoming and still shaping. Still able to love, to impact, and to grow.

And perhaps that's the meaning you've been living all along.

STORIES FROM THE THERAPY ROOM

FELICIA ZEVEN

CHAPTER SIXTY+

Joanna, Seventy-Three

When Joanna first walked into my office, she looked like someone who had been carrying far too much for far too long. Her shoulders were drawn inward, her eyes carried a constant wetness, and her voice trembled when she spoke. At seventy-three, she had recently lost her husband to a sudden heart attack, and only a few months earlier, she had undergone surgery on her knees. She told me she had come to therapy because she was "stuck in mourning" and felt filled with regret.

The very first words she said in our initial session were:

I shouldn't have moved us. If we had stayed in our house, maybe things would be different. He should still be here.

Her guilt was sharp, as if it were holding her hostage. She blamed herself not only for the move but for a lifetime of choices—or rather, what she described as the absence of choices. Joanna had spent decades as a devoted wife and mother, raising four children in a large house filled with chores, routines, and responsibilities. Looking back, she felt that she had lived according to others' expectations: her parents, her husband, and later, her children. *I don't even know who I am without them*, she said.

Unravelling the Past

In our first sessions, we began gently tracing the roots of these feelings. I asked Joanna about her upbringing, and it became clear that silence about emotions had always been the background music of her life. Both she and her late husband grew up in households where feelings were never discussed. Her parents had stressed hard work, discipline, and duty. *My mother always told me, "Don't dream too much; it only leads to disappointment." So I didn't*, Joanna confessed one afternoon, her voice tinged with both sadness and recognition.

The same pattern had carried over into her marriage. She and her husband had rarely spoken about fears, longings, or even their own vulnerabilities. Life was structured: she cared for the children, he worked, and when the children left home, they each retreated into separate worlds—he into his hobbies, she into her garden. *We were comfortable, I suppose*, she said once. *But I realise now, we were strangers in some ways. I never told him about my worries of growing older, or about my knees, or even the thoughts I had about death. And he never told me about feeling tired. I saw it in him, but we didn't speak.*

Her children, raised in that same atmosphere, also learned to keep their feelings quiet. After her husband's death, Joanna found herself surrounded by family yet feeling profoundly alone. Babysitting her grandchildren, she often compared their households to her own and felt increasingly disconnected from both her past and her present.

Sitting with Grief

Our early work was centred on mourning. Joanna needed space to grieve—not just her husband, but the life she thought she had, and the possibilities she had never pursued. Together, we worked on allowing her sadness to exist without judgement and on bringing compassion to herself.

I remember one session when Joanna sobbed as she said:

I wasted my life. I could have studied, I could have travelled, I could have sung . . . but I did none of it. And now it's too late.

I asked her softly, "If you imagine speaking to yourself as if you were one of your grandchildren, what would you say?"

She hesitated, then whispered: *I'd say . . . you did the best you could, with what you knew. You were a good mother, a good wife.* It was one of the first moments where she allowed a drop of self-compassion to enter the room.

Building Bridges with Her Children

As Joanna grew more open to exploring her past, it became clear that her relationships with her children were also burdened by unspoken tension. They loved their mother deeply, but each carried their own frustrations. Joanna herself often felt dismissed, as though her children did not understand her.

We decided to invite her children to some sessions. These meetings were tense but brought results. The children voiced that they sometimes experienced Joanna as critical or distant. Joanna, in turn, admitted that she didn't always know how to connect with them emotionally, because she had never learned how. Together, they discussed not only the past but also the future—what would happen if Joanna's health declined, what she wanted for herself, and how they could support her. This brought her a surprising sense of peace. "I feel lighter," she said afterward. "I don't have to carry everything alone anymore."

Rediscovering Herself

Once Joanna's grief had been given room to breathe, we began turning toward her values and dreams. Who was Joanna beyond being a wife and mother?

At first, she struggled with the question. Decades of living for others had left her unsure of what she wanted. But slowly, she began to recall long-forgotten desires: she had loved singing as a young girl, she had always wanted to learn French, and she dreamed of travelling on her own, despite her fears.

We worked together on breaking these dreams into steps. She joined a local choir, her heart racing the first evening she walked into the hall. To her surprise, she was welcomed warmly, and within weeks, she was laughing with her new choir friends. *I haven't laughed like this in years*, she told me, her eyes shining.

She made a habit of visiting her neighbours every Tuesday, finding comfort in new companionship. She took courage and planned a trip by car to a nearby city. In therapy, we rehearsed each detail: what she would do if she couldn't find the hotel, how she would manage parking, how she could soothe herself if loneliness struck. Preparing this way gave her a sense of agency she hadn't felt in decades.

And then there was French. Joanna signed up for a beginner's course and proudly showed me her first sentences in the language. *It makes me feel alive again*, she said, *like I'm still growing*.

A New Voice

Over the months, Joanna transformed. Her grief remained—grief never truly disappears—but it was no longer the only story she carried. She began to weave in new threads: curiosity, connection, and self-discovery.

One afternoon, during our final sessions, she reflected:

All my life, I thought I wasn't allowed to choose. Now I see I can. I can choose to sing, to travel, to learn. I can choose to live, even without him. I will always miss him, but I don't have to disappear with him.

Joanna's journey was not about erasing her past. It was about embracing it with compassion, understanding how it shaped her, and then gently stepping into a future that still held possibility. She left therapy not with all her questions answered, but with a new voice—one that was finally her own.

Michael, Sixty-One

When Michael, aged sixty-one, sat down in my office for the first time, his presence carried both strength and exhaustion. He was broad-shouldered, strong, the kind of man who still went to the gym several times a week. His posture was upright, his handshake firm, his movements deliberate. On the outside, he looked like someone who had weathered life with resilience. But his eyes revealed the wear of decades of pushing himself to meet expectations that were never really his own.

He told me, almost in a whisper, *I don't know what to do with myself anymore. I've worked all my life to prove I was enough, and now, with retirement coming closer, I feel like I'm going to disappear.*

Michael came into therapy with a tangle of burdens: the scars of an upbringing where achievement mattered more than love, a marriage marked by resentment, children who blamed him for his absence, and an uncertain future without the identity of work.

Growing Up Under Pressure

As we explored his childhood, Michael described a father who was powerful and intimidating—a man who had built a chain of supermarkets and demanded perfection from his son. *He never hugged me. Never once*, Michael said, his voice shaking. *All I remember him saying was that I wasn't trying hard enough, that I was weak.*

His mother, though present, was passive and compliant, always siding with his father: *She didn't defend me. She just told me to listen, to behave, to be grateful.*

Michael internalised a message early on: his worth depended on success. Feelings had no place in his childhood home.

Following his father's path, he joined the family business, even though he never felt at home there. *I was pretending every day*, he admitted. *I wore the suit, I made the deals, but inside I was empty. Still, I kept going. I thought maybe one day he'd say he was proud of me.*

That day never came.

Marriage and Family Life

In his twenties, Michael met Sofia, a woman from abroad who had fallen in love with his energy and ambition. She left her country, her language, and her family behind to be with him. But the reality of their marriage was difficult.

Michael worked endlessly to keep up with his father's expectations. At home, he was irritable, quick-tempered, and emotionally absent. Sofia carried the weight of raising their two children alone in a foreign land. *I felt like I was always walking on eggshells*, she later said when she joined him for therapy.

Michael admitted that in those years, he hardly noticed how isolated she was. *I was so wrapped up in proving myself at work, I didn't see what was happening in my own home*, he said with tears in his eyes. The children grew up resenting him. They remembered him as the father who came home late, who shouted when he was tired, and who was emotionally distant.

Collapse and Turning Point

In his mid-fifties, Michael's façade began to crumble. He suffered burnout and depression. Leaving the supermarket business was both a relief and a crisis—without the work that had defined him, he felt hollow.

But something unexpected happened. Searching for purpose, he volunteered at a centre for autistic teenagers. Slowly, he discovered a part of himself that had been buried for decades. He found he had patience, tenderness, and creativity—qualities he had never been allowed to show in his father's world. *When I'm with those kids, I don't feel like I'm failing. I feel . . . enough*, he said in one session, his face lighting up for the first time.

Facing the Past

Despite this new chapter, Michael carried heavy burdens: his wife's deep resentment, his children's anger, and his own fear of ageing and retirement. In therapy, we worked step by step. We began with his past. I suggested he write a letter to his father—though his father had long passed away. At first, he resisted: *What's the point? He won't read it.*

I explained that the letter wasn't for his father, but for him. Weeks later, Michael came back with trembling hands and read it aloud:

You never saw me. You never told me I was enough. I worked every day to make you proud, and you never were. I'm done carrying your voice inside me. From now on, I decide who I am.

When he finished, he cried deeply—tears that had been waiting since boyhood. *I feel lighter*, he whispered. *Like I've been carrying a backpack of stones, and I just put it down.*

Healing Relationships

We then invited Sofia into the sessions. The air was heavy when she spoke. She expressed her loneliness, her years of silence, her anger at being abandoned emotionally. Michael listened—at first defensively, then with growing humility. *I didn't realise how alone you were*, he admitted. *I thought I was working for all of us, but I see now—I wasn't really there.*

These conversations were painful, but also opened a door. They didn't erase the past, but they allowed Sofia to feel heard and Michael to take responsibility.

Sessions with his children were equally raw. They voiced their pain: the birthdays missed, the fear of his anger, the absence of a father they longed for. Michael apologised, not with excuses, but with sincerity: *I can't change what I didn't give you then. But I want to be here for you now, if you'll let me.*

Reclaiming Himself

We also focused on Michael's fear of retirement. For a man who had always been defined by work, the thought of stepping away felt like disappearing. But together, we explored his values—what truly mattered to him beyond the old pursuit of success.

He realised that the work with autistic children wasn't just a hobby—it was a calling. He decided to continue, even after retirement, as a mentor and volunteer. He also reconnected with physical vitality, continuing to go to the gym but with a new mindset: not to prove his strength, but to care for his body.

For the first time in his life, Michael began practicing emotional openness. He allowed himself to cry in therapy, to admit when he felt scared, to share softer feelings with his wife and children. *It feels strange*, he said once, smiling, *but also freeing. Like I don't have to "man up" anymore.*

CHAPTER 12: THE MEANING OF LIFE—A CONVERSATION WORTH HAVING

A New Chapter

When our sessions drew to a close, Michael reflected on his journey:

All my life, I chased approval. I wanted to prove I was good enough—for my father, for my family, for the world. But I see now—it was never about proving. It's about being. With those kids, with my wife, with my children . . . I just want to be present. That's enough.

Michael's story was not about undoing the past, but about reclaiming his present. By letting go of his father's voice, by facing the pain in his marriage and family, and by embracing his newfound calling, he began writing a second beginning for himself—one shaped not by pressure, but by authenticity.

Evelyn, Seventy

Evelyn was seventy, though she carried herself as if she had lived several lifetimes already. When she first entered my office, she was elegantly dressed—her silver hair perfectly cut, a long scarf wrapped around her shoulders, her nails painted a soft shade of red. There was dignity in her posture, but also a fragile weariness.

She sat down and smiled politely before speaking, her voice calm but steady:

I've lived a full life, at least on the outside. But when I go home at night, it's just me, four walls, and silence. And I can't seem to escape the thought: what will happen to me when I'm older, weaker, and no one is around?

A Lifetime of Relationships That Didn't Last

In our early sessions, Evelyn spoke about her history of relationships. She had never married and had no children. Over the years, she had dated both men and women, sometimes drawn to passion, sometimes to stability, but never managing to build something lasting.

I was always looking for a kind of love that could hold me, she said once. *But it was always either too much or not enough. I don't regret loving who I loved—but I do regret not finding someone to really grow old with.*

Some relationships had burned brightly but ended in betrayal; others faded slowly into distance. Each ending left her with a deeper ache, one that accumulated quietly over time.

A Life Abroad

Evelyn had also lived abroad during parts of her life. She spent years in Spain in her thirties, working for an international publishing house, and later lived in Paris for nearly a decade. She spoke about the excitement of building a life in a new culture, of falling in and out of love, of creating circles of friends from all over the world.

But with each return home, the contrast grew sharper. She came back with stories and experiences, but also with the reminder that her roots were shallow. *I have friends scattered across countries*, she told me. *But when I need someone close by—to help if I fall, or just to share a meal—there's often no one.*

The Ache of Loneliness

As we explored further, it became clear that Evelyn's deepest struggle was with loneliness. She lived alone in a small apartment in the city, her days filled with errands, books, and the occasional coffee with a friend. But her evenings stretched endlessly.

I hate Sundays, she said once. *It's the day couples go for walks, families gather. I sit by the window and watch people going by, and it feels like I'm on the outside of life looking in.*

The loneliness was amplified by fears about ageing. With no children or close family nearby, Evelyn often asked herself who would care for her if she became ill, who would visit her in a hospital, or who would make decisions on her behalf. These worries became louder at night, leaving her sleepless and anxious.

Tracing the Roots

In therapy, we traced these patterns back to her upbringing. Evelyn was the youngest of three, raised in a household where achievement was valued above emotional expression. Her father was distant, her mother preoccupied with her own struggles.

I don't think I ever knew what stability felt like, she said. *So I looked for it everywhere—in men, in women, in countries, in jobs. But I never found a place where I could just rest.*

Reframing the Present

Our work together focused on two intertwined threads: her relationship with herself and her relationship with others.

First, we began cultivating compassion for the life she had lived. Instead of framing her past only in terms of "failures," Evelyn began to see it as a complex story—one where she had made choices with the tools she had, and where richness existed alongside loss.

I used to tell myself I wasted my life, she said one day. *Now I can see that it wasn't wasted—it was different. I've loved, I've travelled, I've worked hard. Maybe it just doesn't look like the picture I once imagined.*

Second, we worked on practical steps to reduce her isolation. Evelyn joined a local book club, which gave her not only intellectual stimulation but also regular social contact. She also started volunteering at a community centre, helping younger women with writing and job applications. *It gives me a sense of being useful*, she said with gentle pride.

Exploring Ageing with Courage

In our sessions, we also faced Evelyn's fears about ageing and vulnerability. She decided to create an advance care plan, naming a close friend as her proxy decision-maker. Though difficult, this conversation gave her more peace of mind.

We also worked on embracing activities that brought her joy. She took up painting again, something she had loved in her twenties but abandoned during the busy years of work and travel. To her surprise, she found herself lost in colour for hours, feeling both calm and alive.

One of the most transformative moments came when she realised she didn't have to see herself only through the lens of what she lacked. *I'm not just the woman who never married or had children*, she said in one session, her eyes brightening. *I'm the woman who has friends in three countries, who still loves to learn, who can reinvent herself at seventy.*

A New Kind of Belonging

By the end of our time together, Evelyn's loneliness hadn't disappeared—but she was no longer consumed by it. She was painting again, laughing with her book club, and even planning a short trip back to Spain, this time not chasing love, but reconnecting with a part of herself.

On our final session, she smiled and said:

I used to think I was always on the outside of life. Now I see that I've been living life all along—it just didn't look like anyone else's. And I still have time to make it meaningful.

Evelyn's story was not one of finding the perfect partner or solving loneliness completely. Nor was it about "fixing" her life into a conventional shape. It was about courage: the courage to face herself honestly, to soften the weight of regret, and to create belonging in her own way.

AFTERWORD

Well . . . here we are. You made it to the end. Which, if you think about it, is already proof of something quite extraordinary: you're still curious. You're still willing to sit with new ideas, wrestle with old ones, and do exercises that might have felt a bit awkward at first. That alone deserves applause. Please take a moment to acknowledge and appreciate yourself. I mean it.

When I began writing this book, my hope was simple but big: to walk beside you through some deeply personal territory, and to make therapy feel less like stepping into a cold, clinical office and more like having a thoughtful conversation over tea and cookies. I wanted to demystify the process, strip away the jargon, and show you that working on yourself is not about "fixing" something broken; it's about gently polishing what's already there. And yes, even at this stage of life, there is still plenty of polishing to be done.

If you've followed along and done the exercises (or even if you just *thought* about doing them; thinking counts as an entry-level warm-up), you've already given yourself something precious: *attention*. You've stopped to examine the threads of your own story—the values and roles that shaped you, the beliefs that may have once been helpful but now feel like ill-fitting shoes. That's no small thing. Because so much of life—especially later in life—can slip into autopilot. And this? This was you retaking the wheel.

In the second part of our journey together, we went into some tender places: retirement, grief, physical changes, loneliness, and the meaning of life. These are not "light reading" topics, but they are *real*. They are the kinds of things we often carry quietly, sometimes believing no one else could understand. But you are not alone; not in your fears, not in your questions, and certainly not in your longing for meaning. The fact that you've read these chapters tells me you are someone who still seeks connection and clarity, even when life feels uncertain.

Here's the truth I most want to leave you with: it is never too late to grow. I have seen people in their seventies challenge long-held regrets and forgive themselves for things they thought they'd carry forever. I have seen people in their eighties discover new hobbies, make new friends, and even (to their own surprise) fall in love again. Change doesn't require a perfect body, or a blank calendar, or a flawless mental health history. It just requires willingness.

So please don't let anyone, including yourself, tell you, *This is just the way I am now.* You are still allowed to rewrite old narratives, shift perspectives, drop burdens, and open new doors. You are still allowed to surprise yourself.

If this book has, in any way, helped you do that, whether by making you a little kinder to yourself, a little more forgiving of your past, a little less weighed down by guilt, or simply a little more hopeful, then I am already overjoyed. If it has made you laugh at least once while thinking deeply, even better. Humour and insight are a fine pair of travelling companions.

As for me, this is my very first published self-help book. Which means I am wide open to feedback: what resonated with you, what you wished there was more of, and what you feel is still missing in conversations about later life. I am already gathering ideas for future books on related topics, but I would much rather write something you actually *need* than something I just *think* you might need. If you'd like to share your thoughts, your story, or just say hello, you can find me through my website: **www.chapter60.online**. Reviews are also very much appreciated.

Thank you for trusting me enough to take this journey. Thank you for letting me into your thoughts, your memories, and your hopes. I have enormous respect for the courage it takes to turn the mirror inward, especially at a stage of life when many people feel they *should* have everything figured out by now. That's the secret, though: no one ever has it all figured out. And that's not failure; that's being human.

So, as we close this chapter together, I'll leave you with this: You are not done. Your story is still unfolding, and you are still the author. The pen is in your hand. Use it. Write with curiosity. Write with kindness. And write without fear of crossing out a line and starting again.

From one human to another,

Thank you for letting me walk this part of the road with you.

Printed in France by Amazon
Brétigny-sur-Orge, FR

40208447R00087